J. R. R. Tolkien's

THE HOBBIT

Teacher Guide

MEMORIA PRESS

MEMORIA PRESS
www.MemoriaPress.com

J. R. R. Tolkien's
THE HOBBIT

TEACHER GUIDE
Contributing Editors: Cheryl Lowe, Brett Vaden, Sean Brooks

ISBN 978-1-61538-065-7

Cover Illustration: Daniel Young

Contents

Teaching Guidelines ... 4
Introduction: J. R. R. Tolkien ... 7
Chapter 1: An Unexpected Party ... 8
The Dwarves' Song ... 10
Poetry Week One: Verses 1-3 ... 11
Poetry Week Two: Verses 4-6 ... 12
Poetry Week Three: Verses 7-10 ... 13
Chapter 2: Roast Mutton ... 14
Chapter 3: A Short Rest ... 16
Chapter 4: Over Hill and Under Hill ... 18
Chapter 5: Riddles in the Dark ... 20
Chapter 6: Out of the Frying-Pan into the Fire ... 22
Chapter 7: Queer Lodgings ... 24
Chapter 8: Flies and Spiders ... 26
Chapter 9: Barrels Out of Bond ... 28
Chapter 10: A Warm Welcome ... 30
Chapter 11: On the Doorstep ... 32
Chapter 12: Inside Information ... 34
Chapter 13: Not at Home ... 36
Chapter 14: Fire and Water ... 38
Chapter 15: The Gathering of the Clouds ... 40
Chapter 16: A Thief in the Night ... 42
Chapter 17: The Clouds Burst ... 44
Chapter 18: The Return Journey ... 46
Chapter 19: The Last Stage ... 48

APPENDIX
Book Notes: Dwarves ... 53
Book Notes: Characters ... 54
Book Notes: Creature List ... 55
Book Notes: Places ... 56
Book Notes: Adventures ... 57
Book Notes: Summaries ... 58
Spelling / Usage ... 59
Runic Alphabet ... 60
Runic Alphabet Translation ... 61
The Story Behind a Name ... 62
The Story of Your Name ... 63
Inside Information ... 64

DISCUSSION QUESTIONS ANSWER KEY ... 68

QUIZZES & TESTS ... 73

QUIZZES & TESTS KEY ... 99

PREPARING TO READ:

REVIEW

- Orally review any previous vocabulary.
- Review the plot of the book as read so far.
- Periodically review the concepts of character, setting, and plot.

STUDY GUIDE PREVIEW

- Reading Notes:
    - Read aloud together.
    - This section gives the student key characters, places, and terms that are relevant to a particular time period, etc.
- Vocabulary:
    - Read aloud together so that students will recognize words when they come across them in their reading.
    - Look at each word within the context that it is used, and help your student come up with the best synonym that defines the word. (Make sure it is a synonym the student knows the meaning of.)
    - Record the word's meaning in the students' study guides. (Use students' knowledge of Latin and other vocabulary to decipher meanings.)
- Comprehension Questions:
    - Read through these questions with students to encourage purposeful reading.

READING:

- Student reads the chapter (or selection of the chapter for that lesson) independently or to the teacher (for younger students).
- For younger students, you can alternate between teacher-read and student-read passages. Model good reading skills. Encourage students to read expressively and smoothly. The teacher may occasionally take oral reading grades.
- While reading, mark each vocabulary word as you come across it.
- Have students take note in their study guide margin of pages where a Comprehension Question is answered.

AFTER READING:

COMPREHENSION QUESTIONS

- Older students can answer these questions independently, but younger students (2nd-4th) need to answer the questions orally, form a good sentence, and then write it down, using correct punctuation, capitalization, and spelling. (You may want to write the sentence down for the younger student after forming it orally, and then let the student copy it perfectly.)
- It is not necessary to write the answer to every question; some may be better answered orally. Just make sure you answer the questions that will appear on tests so that students will have the information they need to study.
- Answering questions and composing answers is a valuable learning activity. Questions require students to think; writing a concise answer is a good composition exercise.

QUOTATIONS AND DISCUSSION QUESTIONS

- Use the Quotations and Discussion Questions section of each lesson as a guide to your oral discussion of the key concepts in the chapter that may not be covered in the comprehension questions.
- These talking points can take your oral discussion to a higher level than covered in the students' written work. Use this time as an opportunity to introduce higher-level thinking. You can introduce concepts the students may not be mature enough to fully understand yet but that would be beneficial for them to begin thinking about.
- A key to the Discussion Questions is in the back of the *Teacher Guide*.

ENRICHMENT

- The Enrichment activities include composition, copywork, dictation, research, mapping, drawing, poetry work, literary terms, and more.
- This section has a variety of activities in it, but the most valuable activity is composition. Your student should complete at least one composition assignment each week. Proof student's work and have student copy composition until grammatically perfect. Insist on clear, concise writing. For younger students, start with 2-3 sentences, and do the assignment together. The student can form good sentences orally as you write them down, and then the student copies them.
- These activities can be completed as time and interest allow. Do not feel you need to complete all of these activities. Choose the ones that you feel are the best use of your students' time.

UNIT REVIEW AND TESTS

- There is a unit review and a quiz or test following every few lessons (varies by individual guide).
- On the weeks that have these reviews and tests, you may want to do the review early in the week, and then drill it orally a couple of times before giving the test at the end of the week.
- A final comprehensive test is also included.
- Vocabulary Terms, Comprehension Questions, and Quotations with an asterisk in the *Teacher Guide* indicate important plot points that will appear on the quizzes and tests.

Introduction: J. R. R. Tolkien

John Ronald Reuel Tolkien lived from 1892 until 1973. His lifetime included the rise of the automobile and motion pictures, World Wars I and II, the discovery of atomic energy, the beginning of space exploration, and the first computers. John Ronald, however, was not as attracted to the new world of machines and technology as he was to an older world—the world that contained the English countryside where he grew up, the world that held the stories and myths he loved to read (and write) about, and the world of simple things he enjoyed, such as good food, gardening, and the fellowship of close friends.

Tolkien held a special enjoyment for language. He loved words, and he was fascinated by the way they worked and the stories they could tell. When he was a boy, he learned several languages from his mother, including Latin. He enjoyed reading stories like *Peter Pan* and *Alice in Wonderland*, but he liked fairy stories most of all, especially the "Curdie" stories of George MacDonald and *The Red Fairy Book*, by Andrew Lang. Tolkien grew to be so interested in words that he became a philologist, a scholar who studies languages and literature. During his years of university at Oxford, Tolkien not only started writing poetry, but he invented two languages, which he said came from elves. Behind his love for language was an imagination so big, it went further than poetry or story to the realm of mythology.

Before Tolkien got very far creating his mythical world, he was summoned by the British army to fight in World War I. While serving in the muddy trenches of France, he thought more about his mythology, both to continue his creative work and to escape the bloody horror of war with his mind. Two of Tolkien's best friends also fought in the trenches, and during the Battle of the Somme they were killed. Tolkien himself was wounded by a mortar shell and had to be sent back to England, where he spent many months recovering from his injuries and other illnesses. It was in large part because of the friends he lost in the war that Tolkien was inspired to make his mythology a lifelong work.

Several other important people inspired Tolkien, including his wife, Edith (whom he called "Luthien," after an elf princess he created), his good friend and colleague C. S. Lewis, and his four children: John, Michael, Christopher, and Priscilla. Tolkien loved his children very much, and he enjoyed using his stories to entertain them. One of these stories took place "long ago in the quiet of the world," a time when elves, goblins, and dragons lived. The story was about a little person who goes on a grand adventure, and it was quite entertaining. It was so good, in fact, that it was published in 1937, and since that time, it has become a classic of children's fiction. Tolkien thought that no child ought read a book that an adult would not enjoy. And so, as you will find if you keep reading *The Hobbit*, it is a book that can both entertain and teach a person their whole life long.

Chapter 1: An Unexpected Party

"In a hole in the ground there lived a hobbit."

READING NOTES

Bilbo Baggins	well-to-do hobbit living at The Hill in Hobbiton
The Bagginses	hobbit family respected for their wealth and sensibleness
hobbits	little people, half the height of humans, who relish comfort
The Tooks	hobbit family living across The Water; known for adventures
Gandalf	wizard who knew Bilbo's grandfather, the Old Took
dwarves	people of short, stout stature, with beards and a love of treasure
Thorin	important dwarf leading a band of twelve other dwarves
Smaug	dragon who stole the dwarves' home and treasure

VOCABULARY: Write the meaning of each bold word or phrase.

1. Mr. Baggins was not quite so **prosy** as he liked to believe adj. commonplace, dull
2. who was feeling positively **flummoxed** adj. bewildered, confused
3. the **depredations** of dragons n. plunderings
4. Thorin with his feet on the **fender** n. fireplace screen
5. this most excellent and **audacious** hobbit adj. fearlessly bold, fearless
6. The **estimable** Mr. Baggins adj. worthy of esteem
7. **singed** beards adj. scorched; surface-burned

COMPREHENSION QUESTIONS: Answer the following in complete sentences.

1. The Tooks are richer than the Bagginses, but not as respectable. Why?

   One of the Took ancestors is said to have taken a fairy wife, and they are known for going on adventures.

2. What are the dwarves planning to do?

   The dwarves plan to win back their home and gold from the dragon Smaug.

3. Gandalf says Bilbo is "as fierce as a dragon in a pinch." Why does Gandalf say this?

Gandalf is trying to assure the dwarves that Bilbo will be of use to them, and he also knows more of Bilbo's abilities than Bilbo does.

4. Why does Gandalf choose Bilbo?

Gandalf trusts in Bilbo's Tookish qualities. (And Bilbo makes a lucky fourteen to add to the dwarves' thirteen.)

5. Does Thorin have faith in Bilbo? How can you tell?

Thorin doesn't have faith in Bilbo. He seems to guess that Bilbo is not a real burglar and that he is timid of adventures. He catches Bilbo speaking as if he were not going on the journey.

QUOTATIONS

Gandalf 1. *"I am looking for someone to share in an adventure that I am arranging, and it's very difficult to find anyone."*

Bilbo 2. *"We are plain quiet folk and I have no use for adventures. Nasty disturbing uncomfortable things! Make you late for dinner!"*

Gloin 3. *"He looks more like a grocer than a burglar!"*

Bilbo 4. *"Tell me what you want done, and I will try it, if I have to walk from here to the East of East and fight the wild Were-worms in the Last Desert."*

DISCUSSION QUESTIONS

1. Explain why the second and fourth quotations show us two different sides of the speaker.
2. From where have the dwarves first come? Why did they move south?
3. Describe the glory days of the dwarves and their relationship with the men of Dale.
4. Explain the decline in the work and prestige of the dwarves as they changed from craftsmen to blacksmiths to coal miners.

ENRICHMENT

1. Read Thorin's story aloud in class (beginning with "O very well," and ending with "the rightful heir"). Write a one-paragraph summary of the history of the dwarves.
2. Begin filling in the Book Notes in the Appendix.

The Dwarves' Song

1
Far over the misty mountains cold
To dungeons deep and caverns old,
We must away ere break of day,
To seek the pale enchanted gold.

2
The dwarves of yore made mighty spells,
While hammers fell like ringing bells
In places deep, where dark things sleep,
In hollow halls beneath the fells.

3
For ancient king and elvish lord
There many a gleaming golden hoard
They shaped and wrought, and light they caught
To hide in gems on hilt of sword.

4
On silver necklaces they strung
The flowering stars, on crowns they hung
The dragon-fire, in twisted wire
They meshed the light of moon and sun.

5
Far over the misty mountains cold
To dungeons deep and caverns old,
We must away ere break of day,
To claim our long-forgotten gold.

6
Goblets they carved there for themselves
And harps of gold; where no man delves
There lay they long, and many a song
Was sung unheard by men or elves.

7
The pines were roaring on the height,
The winds were moaning in the night.
The fire was red, it flaming spread;
The trees like torches blazed with light.

8
The bells were ringing in the dale
And men looked up with faces pale;
Then dragon's ire more fierce than fire
Laid low their towers and houses frail.

9
The mountain smoked beneath the moon;
The dwarves, they heard the tramp of doom.
They fled their hall to dying fall
Beneath his feet, beneath the moon.

10
Far over the misty mountains grim
To dungeons deep and caverns dim,
We must away ere break of day,
To win our harps and gold from him!

Poetry Week One: Verses 1-3

VOCABULARY: Write the meaning of each bold word or phrase.

1. We must away **ere** break of day before
2. The dwarves of **yore** times long past
3. In hollow halls beneath the **fells** mountains or hills
4. here many a gleaming golden **hoard** hidden funds
5. They shaped and **wrought** put together; worked
6. To hide in gems on **hilt** of sword handle

COMPREHENSION QUESTIONS: Answer the following in complete sentences.

1. What were the dwarves' mighty spells?

   The spells were the dwarves' craft of making beautiful things from precious metals and gems, the beauty of which casts spells over men and other races.

2. Paraphrase: "... and light they caught / to hide in gems on hilt of sword."

   The dwarves' magic method of cutting and setting gems to make them catch light and reflect it makes the gems and gold seem to capture light.

3. What item did the "dwarves of yore" make, out of what materials, and for whom?

   They made swords and other things from precious metals and gems for ancient kings and elvish lords.

4. Rewrite verses 1-3 in prose.

   Example: At the break of day we must go to seek pale enchanted gold far over the cold misty mountains to deep dungeons and old caverns. In times long past the dwarves made mighty spells in hollow halls beneath the hills. They hammered in deep places where dark things sleep. There they shaped and wrought gold for ancient kings and elvish lords, and they cut and fashioned gems on the hilts of swords.

Poetry Week Two: Verses 4-6

VOCABULARY: Write the meaning of each bold word or phrase.

1. **Goblets** they carved for themselves cups
2. Where no man **delves** digs; searches

COMPREHENSION QUESTIONS: Answer the following in complete sentences.

1. What are "flowering stars"? "dragon-fire"?

   The flowering stars are jewels (perhaps sapphires or diamonds); dragon-fire is gold.

2. What were the dwarves claiming besides their gold?

   They claimed their lost kingdom and heritage—the title of King under the Mountain.

3. What do harps and goblets symbolize?

   They symbolize music and feasting, prosperity and ease, and the king's glorious reign.

4. Do you think the dwarves became overconfident of their wealth?

   Yes.

5. Rewrite verses 4-6 in prose.

   Example: They strung jewels on silver necklaces, and they hung gold on crowns. They meshed the light of moon and sun in twisted wire. At the break of day we must go far over the cold misty mountains to claim our long-forgotten gold in deep dungeons and old caverns. They carved goblets and gold harps for themselves. They laid for a long time where no one goes, and they sang many songs that have never been heard by men or elves.

Poetry Week Three: Verses 7-10

VOCABULARY: Write the meaning of each bold word or phrase.

1. The bells were ringing in the **dale** valley
2. Then dragon's **ire** more fierce than fire anger

COMPREHENSION QUESTIONS: Answer the following in complete sentences.

1. What happens in verses 7 & 8? Why?

   The dragon came from the North, flew over the trees, and set them on fire.

2. What happens in verse 9? What was the "tramp of doom"?

   The dwarves heard the dragon coming (tramp of doom) and fled.

3. Why did the dwarves leave their hall? What happened?

   They heard the destruction of Lake-town and Dale, and of the dragon's approach; they knew he was headed for their treasure. They left to escape and possibly to fight; the dragon killed them as they were feasting.

4. Who is "him" in the last line of verse 10?

   Smaug, the new King under the Mountain

5. Does dragon-fire attract dragons?

   Yes— "dragon's ire more fierce than fire"; the dwarves' greed lured the dragon's greed.

6. Identify the three verses in the entire poem that are nearly identical. Copy the last line of each. When read together, what story do they tell?

   They are verses 1, 5, and 10: "To seek the pale enchanted gold," "To claim our long-forgotten gold," "To win our harps and gold from him!" They tell of the yearning for and resolution to recover the gold and the old way of life.

7. Rewrite verses 7-10 in prose.

   Example: The high pine trees were on fire, and the wind spread the flames. In the dale, alarm bells were ringing, and the men saw the dragon, who destroyed their towers and houses. As the fire smoked, the dwarves heard the dragon approaching. They tried to escape but were killed. At the break of day we must go far over the grim misty mountains to deep dungeons and dim caverns to win back our treasure from the dragon.

Chapter 2: Roast Mutton

"... he began to feel that adventures were not so bad after all."

READING NOTES

trolls large creatures; not very clever, but dangerous and evil

VOCABULARY: Write the meaning of each bold word or phrase.

1. funeral expenses to be **defrayed** v. paid, provided payment
2. Thinking it unnecessary to disturb your **esteemed** repose adj. highly regarded, respected
3. proceeded in advance to make **requisite** preparations adj. necessary, obligatory
4. parcels and **paraphernalia** n. miscellaneous items, equipment
5. a nice bit o' fat valley **mutton** n. flesh of sheep used as food
6. **purloined** the beer v. stole, robbed
7. Gandalf tried various **incantations** n. spells, chants

COMPREHENSION QUESTIONS: Answer the following in complete sentences.

1. What causes Bilbo to leave his hobbit hole without a pocket-handkerchief?

   Thorin's letter and Gandalf pushing him out the door cause Bilbo to leave without his pocket-handkerchief.

2. Where does Bilbo meet the Company of dwarves?

   He meets them at the Inn of the Green Dragon.

3. What is the Company's first mishap?

   A pony falls in while fording a river; supplies are lost.

4. Where does the Company encounter the trolls?

   They encounter the trolls at night in the dreary hills while making camp.

5. What is Bilbo's discovery about himself?

"He had read of a good many things he had neither seen nor done."

6. What happens to trolls at daybreak?

They turn to stone.

7. What does the Company find in the trolls' lair?

They find supplies, elven swords, and gold. They take the supplies and swords and bury the gold.

QUOTATIONS

Gandalf 1. *"Great Elephants! You are not at all yourself this morning—you have never dusted the mantelpiece!"*

Dwalin 2. *"You will have to manage without pocket-handkerchiefs, and a good many other things, before you get to the journey's end."*

Bilbo 3. *"Bother burgling and everything to do with it! I wish I was at home in my nice hole by the fire, with the kettle just beginning to sing!"*

William 4. *"Blimey, Bert, look what I've copped!"*

Bilbo 5. *"I am a good cook myself, and cook better than I cook, if you see what I mean."*

DISCUSSION QUESTIONS

1. Describe what is happening in the drawing in this chapter.
2. Is Bilbo an optimist or a pessimist? Find specific phrases to support your answer.
3. Compare Thorin's and Gandalf's attempts at rescuing the dwarves. Who is successful? Why?
4. Bilbo is hired as a burglar. What are some hobbit characteristics that fit the job description?

ENRICHMENT

1. Add trolls to your Creature List in the Appendix. Include a description of their appearance, speech, eating habits, their natural habitat, where they had moved to and why, and what happens to them in daylight.

Chapter 3: A Short Rest

"At that moment he felt more tired than he ever remembered feeling before."

READING NOTES

elves	wise and noble people who are also merry and fair
Glamdring	famous elvish sword; "Foe-hammer"; belongs to Gandalf
Orcrist	another famous elvish sword; "Goblin-cleaver"; belongs to Thorin
moon letters	rune letters seen only by special moonlight
Durin's Day	first day of the dwarves' New Year, when the last autumn moon is in the sky

VOCABULARY: Write the meaning of each bold word or phrase.

1. The **bannocks** are baking! n. round, flat griddle cakes
2. uncomfortable, **palpitating** v. pounding, throbbing
3. as **venerable** as a king of dwarves adj. worthy of honor and respect
4. the **remnants** of old robberies n. small remaining quantity, traces
5. **cunning** handwriting adj. clever or deceitful
6. a bit **vexed** adj. angered, irritated

COMPREHENSION QUESTIONS: Answer the following in complete sentences.

1. Where does the Company stop after their encounter with the trolls?

   They stop at the Last Homely House in Rivendell.

2. What do the dwarves think of elves? Why?

   Dwarves think elves are foolish and annoying. Elves tease and laugh at dwarves because of their beards.

3. Describe Elrond.

   Elrond is "as noble and as fair in face as an elf-lord, as strong as a warrior, as wise as a wizard, as venerable as a king of dwarves, and as kind as summer."

4. Who is Durin? Who is his heir?

Durin is the father of the fathers of the eldest race of dwarves, the Longbeards, and is also Thorin's ancestor; Thorin is his heir.

5. What does the moon's light reveal to Elrond? Write the message.

The moon's light reveals a magic rune message written with a silver pen: "Stand by the grey stone when the thrush knocks, and the setting sun with the last light of Durin's Day will shine upon the key-hole."

QUOTATIONS

Bilbo 1. *"Is that The Mountain?"*

Gandalf 2. *"We must not miss the road, or we shall be done for."*

Bilbo 3. *"Hmmm! It smells like elves!"*

Elrond 4. *"Stand by the grey stone when the thrush knocks, and the setting sun with the last light of Durin's Day will shine upon the key-hole."*

DISCUSSION QUESTIONS

1. In the third quotation, where is the speaker when he says this?
2. The adventure with the trolls is not an accident. What does the Company find in the trolls' lair? Where did the swords come from? How does Elrond know? Is this a foreboding that they are on the right road to their quest?

ENRICHMENT

1. Swords are often given names and histories in Tolkien's stories. Compose a paragraph in which you, like Elrond, tell about the name and origin of a sword of your own imagining. Draw your sword.
2. Read the explanation of runes given immediately before Chapter 1 in *The Hobbit*. Then complete the activities found in the Runic Alphabet section in the Appendix.
3. Add to your Book Notes.

Chapter 4: Over Hill and Under Hill

"Though he could not do everything, he could do a great deal for friends in a tight corner."

READING NOTES

goblins cruel, wicked, bad-hearted creatures who live underground

The Great Goblin the ruler of the goblins under the Misty Mountains

VOCABULARY: Write the meaning of each bold word or phrase.

1. the echoes were **uncanny** adj. eerie, mysterious
2. the dwarves were already **yammering** and bleating v. grumbling, complaining
3. **ingenious** devices adj. clever, resourceful
4. wicked dwarves had even made **alliances** with them n. unions, pacts
5. **hordes** of angry goblins n. large groups, crowds

COMPREHENSION QUESTIONS: Answer the following in complete sentences.

1. What is Bilbo's dream? Is he really dreaming?

   Bilbo dreams that a crack in the cave wall opens wider and wider, and then a crack in the floor begins to open up as well. He is dreaming, but when he wakes up, he realizes that the wall really is opening up.

2. Who are the youngest pair of dwarves? Why are they chosen as scouts? How many years younger than the other dwarves are they?

   Fili and Kili are 50 years younger and have the sharpest eyes.

3. Why doesn't Thorin want to tell the goblin king the whole truth about their expedition?

   Goblins would be suspicious of their quest; they would remember stories of the King under the Mountain and would want the treasure.

4. How do the dwarves escape?

Gandalf puts out all the lights in the cavern, kills the Great Goblin with Glamdring, leads the dwarves through the tunnels, and stops with Thorin to fight goblins.

5. What do the goblins fear?

They are afraid of swords Glamdring the Foe-hammer and Orcrist the Goblin-cleaver, which they call Beater and Biter.

6. Who carries Bilbo on his back? What happens?

Dori carries Bilbo on his back. He is grabbed from behind, and Bilbo falls off his back and blacks out.

QUOTATIONS

The Great Goblin	1. *"Who are these miserable persons?"*
Thorin	2. *"We were on a journey to visit our relatives, our nephews and nieces, and first, second, and third cousins, and the other descendants of our grandfathers ..."*
a goblin driver	3. *"He is a liar, O truly tremendous one!"*
Bombur	4. *"Why, O why did I ever bring a wretched little hobbit on a treasure hunt!"*
Gandalf	5. *"Draw your sword, Thorin!"*

DISCUSSION QUESTIONS

1. Describe the drawing in this chapter entitled "The Mountain Path."
2. The first paragraph of this chapter is a metaphor about any adventure or quest in one's life. Explain.
3. "And that was the last time that they used the ponies, packages, baggages, tools and paraphernalia that they had brought with them." To what does this sentence allude? Would they find provisions for the rest of the journey? Explain.
4. Goblins are clever but not creative. What is the purpose of their inventions?

ENRICHMENT

1. Copy the goblins' song in your best penmanship. Make sure you copy it perfectly. This should be copied like a poem, so that each line stands alone. Then memorize it and recite it for an audience.
2. Continue working on your Book Notes.

Chapter 5: Riddles in the Dark

"It was a turning point in his career, but he did not know it."

READING NOTES

Gollum a small, slimy, wicked creature living by the lake down beneath the mountain

The Ring a ring Gollum has possessed for many years that makes its wearer invisible

VOCABULARY: Write the meaning of each bold word or phrase.

1. **throttled** them from behind v. strangled, choked
2. **sheathed** his sword v. holstered, encased
3. **shambling** off at a great pace v. shuffling or hobbling
4. he **ventured** to try v. risked, dared
5. a new strength and **resolve** n. determination, steadfastness

COMPREHENSION QUESTIONS: Answer the following in complete sentences.

1. What does Bilbo find on the floor of the dark tunnel?

   He finds a ring.

2. What comforts Bilbo when he finds he does not have matches to light his pipe?

   He finds his sword.

3. What flummoxes Bilbo?

   He falls into a subterranean lake at the end of the tunnel.

4. Where does Gollum live? Describe his way of life in the lake.

   Gollum lives on an island in the lake; he has a boat, he fishes, and he catches young goblins by throttling them from behind.

5. List some ways that hobbits are not like ordinary people.

   They are used to tunneling underground and have a good sense of direction; they are wise, move quietly, and hide easily.

6. Why does Gollum suggest a game of riddles?

It is the only game he knows, and he wants to find out about Bilbo.

7. Which one of Bilbo's riddles is not really a riddle?

"What have I got in my pocket?"

8. How does Bilbo escape?

The ring makes him invisible, so he follows Gollum secretly and escapes through a stone doorway guarded by goblins.

QUOTATIONS

Bilbo — 1. *"Go back? No good at all! Go sideways? Impossible! Go forward? Only thing to do! On we go!"*

Gollum — 2. *"Is it nice, my preciousss? Is it juicy? Is it scrumptiously crunchable?"*

DISCUSSION QUESTIONS

1. What is the speaker talking about in the second quotation?
2. In narrative form, tell about Bilbo's discovery of the ring, his encounter with Gollum, and his escape.
3. Bilbo and Gollum engage in an ancient riddle game. Can you remember these riddles? Can you make some of your own?

ENRICHMENT

1. Bilbo was hired by the dwarves as a "burglar" although he was given very little information about what that would involve. Has Bilbo been useful in expected ways so far? Is this how the author is showing us that he believes in Providence? Support your position in a short essay with details from the story.

Just by being a hobbit—quiet, not afraid of tunnels, etc.—he finds the ring by accident, but it saves Bilbo and helps him escape.

Chapter 6: Out of the Frying-Pan into the Fire

"Bilbo's reputation went up a very great deal with the dwarves after this."

READING NOTES

wargs evil wolves that live over the Edge of the Wild

eagles proud, strong, noble-hearted birds that live in the Misty Mountains

VOCABULARY: Write the meaning of each bold word or phrase.

1. **abominable** tunnels adj. detestable, loathsome, morally reprehensible
2. He nibbled a bit of **sorrel**. n. plant of the buckwheat family with edible leaves
3. a lonely **pinnacle** of rock n. summit, peak
4. eagle's **eyrie** n. a high perched nest
5. jumping over a **precipice** n. cliff, ledge
6. **famished** with hunger v. starved, exhausted

COMPREHENSION QUESTIONS: Answer the following in complete sentences.

1. What conversation does Bilbo overhear?

   The dwarves and Gandalf debate whether to leave Bilbo or go back to look for him; the dwarves want to leave him, but Gandalf refuses to leave him.

2. What improves Bilbo's reputation?

   His surprise appearance and escape from the goblins impresses the dwarves.

3. How does Gandalf get into the goblins' tunnel?

   When Bilbo yells, Gandalf makes a flash, killing the goblins around him, and nips into the tunnel before it closes.

4. Where does the Company decide to spend the night? What are their misgivings?

   They decide to spend the night in an opening where no trees grow. They have a bad feeling about it and then hear wolves howling.

5. Why are the wolves gathered near the clearing that night? Why are the goblins late?

   The wolves are waiting for the goblins to meet them for a goblin-raid; the death of the Great Goblin has delayed the goblins.

6. With whom are the wargs in alliance? When?

   They are in alliance with the goblins, who ride on their backs, in times of war or for plunder.

7. How is the Company saved?

   The eagles see the commotion from afar and come to the rescue.

QUOTATIONS

Speaker	Quotation
Gandalf	1. *"Mr. Baggins has more about him than you guess."*
Gandalf	2. *"A very ticklish business, it was. Touch and go!"*
Bilbo	3. *"Must we go any further? My toes are all bruised and bent, and my legs ache, and my stomach is wagging like an empty sack."*
Dori	4. *"I can't be always carrying burglars on my back, down tunnels and up trees! What do you think I am? A porter?"*

DISCUSSION QUESTIONS

1. Describe what is shown in the drawing located in this chapter, and tell where a person would be standing if he/she were seeing this view.
2. What about Bilbo is the speaker referring to in the first quotation?
3. Bilbo thinks he has left the dwarves under the mountains; the dwarves think that Bilbo has been left behind. Compare their different reactions to the thought of returning to the goblins' stronghold to search for their lost companions.
4. How does Gandalf settle the issue?
5. Why does Bilbo keep his ring a secret from the dwarves and Gandalf?

ENRICHMENT

1. The goblins' songs are meant to frighten their prey. Dwarves' and elves' songs have a different purpose. Compare and contrast their songs. What do they tell us about the nature of each race? Write your own song. Will it be a goblin song or a dwarf/elf song?

   The goblins are wicked and cruel. The dwarves have a love of home and gold that puts courage into their hearts.

Chapter 7: Queer Lodgings

"Now began the most dangerous part of all the journey."

READING NOTES

Mirkwood a terrible forest; the last peril before the Lonely Mountain

Carrock a rocky island in the Great River built by Beorn

Beorn a good man living near Mirkwood who transforms into a bear

VOCABULARY: Write the meaning of each bold word or phrase.

1. a last **outpost** of the distant mountains n. a detachment set far from the army to prevent surprise
2. your present **plight** n. predicament, unfortunate situation
3. paid little **heed** n. careful attention, regard
4. what is left is out on the **veranda** n. roofed porch
5. the peaks of the mountains **glowered** against the sunset v. stared at angrily, scowled
6. leaves were laid upon the **mould** n. a British word for "ground"

COMPREHENSION QUESTIONS: Answer the following in complete sentences.

1. Why is this chapter titled "Queer Lodgings"? Is there more than one?

   The Company stays in unexpected and unusual lodgings: eagles' eyries and Beorn's lodge.

2. Where and what is the Carrock?

   Carrock is the last outpost of the mountains, a huge slab of stone upon which stone steps have been built by Beorn.

3. Why does Gandalf call Beorn a "skin-changer"?

   Bilbo does not understand Gandalf's meaning at first: Beorn changes into the shape of a great bear at night and patrols his territory.

4. Why does Beorn think kindly of the dwarves? Who are Beorn's enemies?

Beorn thinks kindly of the dwarves because they have killed the Great Goblin. Beorn's enemies are goblins and wargs, or whoever comes too near his home without permission.

5. What does Beorn provide for the Company's continued journey? Is this providential?

He provides ponies and food and water to last for weeks (remember what happened at the beginning of Chapter 6); Yes, this is providential.

6. What is Beorn's advice about Mirkwood? Gandalf's advice?

Beorn's advice: "The way is dark, dangerous, and difficult. Do not go near the enchanted stream. Don't shoot anything. You must not stray from the path." Gandalf's advice: "I'm sending Mr. Baggins with you … this is your expedition; Think of the treasure at the end; forget the forest and the dragon … Don't leave the path!"

QUOTATIONS

Bilbo's eagle — 1. *"Don't pinch! You need not be frightened like a rabbit, even if you look rather like one. It is a fair morning with little wind. What is finer than flying?"*

Gandalf — 2. *"That is Mr. Baggins, a hobbit of good family and unimpeachable reputation."*

Beorn — 3. *"A dozen! That's the first time I've heard eight called a dozen."*

Gandalf — 4. *"Be good, take care of yourselves, and DON'T LEAVE THE PATH!"*

DISCUSSION QUESTIONS

1. Describe what is pictured in the drawing entitled "Beorn's Hall."
2. In the third quotation, what is the speaker talking about?
3. Retell Gandalf's trick of introducing the dwarves to Beorn, two by two. What is Beorn's reaction? How did he practice this same trick with Bilbo in Chapter 1? Compare the two incidents.
4. Describe the area where Beorn lives, and contrast it to Mirkwood forest.

ENRICHMENT

1. You should begin to see that each of the creatures, races, and places have their counterpart in the real world. Make a list of people and places you are familiar with that could be represented by hobbits, goblins, Mirkwood forest, etc.

Chapter 8: Flies and Spiders

"They would soon all have been dead, if it had not been for the hobbit."

READING NOTES

spiders greatly enlarged and wicked spiders that live in Mirkwood

Wood-elves elves who live in the home of the Elvenking in Mirkwood

VOCABULARY: Write the meaning of each bold word or phrase.

1. trees … hung with **lichen** n. moss, fungus
2. horrible pale **bulbous** sort of eyes adj. bulging, spherical
3. the snapped **painter** n. a rope for docking a ship
4. **disquieting** laughter adj. disturbing, troubling
5. They did not care **tuppence** about the butterflies n. two cents
6. the **gloaming** and the dusk n. twilight, evening

COMPREHENSION QUESTIONS: Answer the following in complete sentences.

1. Are the flies referred to in the chapter title literal flies? Explain. List the actual insects encountered by the Company.

   No: the dwarves are the "flies" because they are treated as such by the spiders. The Company encounters black moths, butterflies, and spiders.

2. What happens to Bombur?

   Bombur falls into the enchanted stream when a hart leaps over him. The water casts a spell on him and he falls into a deep sleep.

3. When are the dwarves glad about Beorn's warning to them? When do they later lament the fact that they did not remember his advice?

   The dwarves are thirsty but remember Beorn told them not to touch the water; when Bombur falls in, they realize their danger. Beorn had also warned them not to shoot at anything, but they use all their arrows and later are unable to defend themselves.

4. What finally lures the dwarves off the path? Why and how does it happen?

Hunger and desperation lure them off the path. They see fire from the Wood-elves' feast and hope to get food and help in finding their way out of Mirkwood. This is when they are attacked by spiders.

5. How does Thorin disappear?

He is separated from the others and sleeps through the spider episode. Then he is captured by the Wood-elves, taken to their palace, and placed in the dungeon, where he is fed bread, water, and meat.

QUOTATIONS

Speaker	Quotation
Bombur	1. *"I'm always last and I don't like it. It's somebody else's turn today."*
Thorin	2. *"Don't start grumbling against orders, or something bad will happen to you."*
Thorin	3. *"Is there no end to this accursed forest?"*
Bombur	4. *"Why ever did I wake up! I was having such beautiful dreams."*
Thorin	5. *"You are no joke to carry even after weeks of short commons."*
Bilbo	6. *"I will give you a name and I shall call you Sting."*

DISCUSSION QUESTIONS

1. What is the speaker talking about in the last quotation, and why does he give it this name?
2. Describe the change that comes over Bilbo after his encounter with the spiders. Do you think this would have happened without the ring? Is this why Gandalf told the dwarves that Bilbo could be trusted to take care of them? Is it really the ring or is it Bilbo? Explain.
3. Because the Wood-elves elude and later capture the dwarves, they appear to be hostile. Using the description found in the chapter, summarize the characteristics of this race.

ENRICHMENT

1. Draw a picture of Bilbo in action with his sword.

Chapter 9: Barrels Out of Bond

"At last he had the desperate beginnings of a plan."

READING NOTES

The Elvenking the king of the Wood-elves of Mirkwood; good but stern

VOCABULARY: Write the meaning of each bold word or phrase.

1. They were **surly** and angry adj. bad-tempered, rude
2. the darkest and **remotest** corners adj. secluded, isolated, farthest
3. **potent** wine adj. strong, powerful
4. His fears were quite **justified** adj. shown to be right; vindicated
5. idle **toss-pot** n. drunkard, alcoholic
6. Where the **kine** and oxen feed! n. cows
7. **shingly** shore adj. rocky, rough

COMPREHENSION QUESTIONS: Answer the following in complete sentences.

1. The dwarves are captured by Wood-elves. What are the advantages of this mishap?

   They are taken from the forest and given food and water and kept in the palace.

2. Why do the elves have no need of tying up their prisoners?

   The elves' magic keeps the gates shut; also, the dwarves are so weakened and lost, they make no attempt at escape.

3. What are the crimes the dwarves are accused of committing?

   The dwarves wander in the realm of the Elvenking without leave, use the elves' road, pursue and trouble the elves, and rouse the spiders.

4. How does Bilbo escape capture?

   By wearing his ring, Bilbo stays invisible and trots quietly behind the group.

5. What good results from Bilbo's invisible presence in the Wood-elves' cellar?

Bilbo discovers the only way out of the palace is through the River Gate, and by secretly listening to the elves, he devises a plan of escape.

6. How does Bilbo get possession of the guard's keys?

Bilbo stays by the chief guard and takes the keys when he is drunk with potent wine and falls asleep.

7. What is the weak spot in Bilbo's plan? When is this discovered?

Bilbo has forgotten that someone needs to pack him into a barrel as well as the dwarves. He realizes this at the last minute; he has to ride on a barrel, almost doesn't fit through the tunnel, gets wet, and catches a cold.

QUOTATIONS

Elvenking 1. *"There is no escape from my magic doors for those who are once brought inside."*

Bilbo 2. *"Drat this dwarfish racket!"*

Thorin 3. *"Gandalf spoke true, as usual! A pretty fine burglar you make, it seems, when the time comes."*

all the dwarves 4. *"We shall be bruised and battered to pieces, and drowned too, for certain!"*

DISCUSSION QUESTIONS

1. What plan of Bilbo's are the dwarves referring to in the last quotation?
2. Why does Gandalf leave the Company to fend for themselves? Is Bilbo living up to Gandalf's expectations? Combine information from the previous chapter with the allusions given in this chapter.

ENRICHMENT

1. What do you think would have happened if the Company had stayed on the path and followed all the directions given them by Beorn and Gandalf? Try rewriting this chapter with the Company remaining on the path.

Chapter 10: A Warm Welcome

"I suppose we ought to thank our stars and Mr. Baggins."

READING NOTES

The Long Lake large lake filled by the Running River and Forest River

Dale once-thriving town of men near the Lonely Mountain

Lake-town town of men on the surface of the Long Lake

Master ruler of Lake-town; a shrewd and wary man of business

VOCABULARY: Write the meaning of each bold word or phrase.

1. the stars of the **Wain** were already twinkling n. a wagon; the Big Dipper
2. a **promontory** of rock n. high point of land jutting into water
3. bruised and **buffeted** v. battered, beaten
4. impatient at these **solemnities** n. gravities; serious and dignified feelings
5. wandering **vagabond** dwarves adj. drifting; wandering; aimless
6. wished for no **enmity** with him n. hostility, hate
7. The **quays** were thronged with hurrying feet. n. docks, wharfs

COMPREHENSION QUESTIONS: Answer the following in complete sentences.

1. Why is Bilbo's plan of escape the only route out of Mirkwood?

   The roads have fallen into disuse; the river is the most direct route because of trade with the men.

2. Where do the barrels end their journey?

   The barrels end their journey at Lake-town, near Smaug's stronghold.

3. What can still be seen along the shores of the lake when the water is low?

   The ruins of the original town that Smaug had destroyed can still be seen.

4. Who is the first dwarf to come out of his barrel? How does Bilbo recognize him?

   Thorin comes out first; he is so bedraggled Bilbo only recognizes him by his golden chain and sky-blue hood with the tarnished silver tassel.

5. Why are guards watching the bridge? Why are they not watching very carefully?

   The men have traditionally guarded the bridge from the dragon as they await the return of the King under the Mountain. They are not watching carefully because they do not really think the King will return.

6. What do the townspeople think of the story of Thorin?

   They believe the story immediately and begin feasting and pampering the dwarves and Bilbo.

7. What is the Master of the town thinking about the dwarves' quest? Is he sorry to see them go?

   The Master of the town feels they are not telling the truth but humors them because the townspeople are so excited, and he doesn't want to upset them. He is not sorry to see them go because they are expensive to house and entertain, and the town's business is at a standstill.

QUOTATIONS

Bilbo	1. *"Well, are you alive or are you dead?"*
Fili	2. *"I hope I shall never smell the smell of apples again!"*
scouts of Lake-town	3. *"Who are you and what do you want?"*
Elvenking	4. *"Very well! We'll see! No treasure will come back through Mirkwood without my having something to say in the matter."*

DISCUSSION QUESTIONS

1. Describe the details pictured in the drawing of "Lake Town."
2. In the first quotation, to whom is Bilbo speaking, and why does he ask this question?
3. The men of the town are skeptical of the old legends and put on a pretense of guarding the bridge from the dragon. Is their behavior an allegory of our society's lack of faith?

ENRICHMENT

1. Read "The Story Behind a Name" in the Appendix and complete its exercises.

Chapter 11: On the Doorstep

"At last unexpectedly they found what they were seeking."

READING NOTES

Ravenhill a watchtower height on the southern spur of the mountain

Front Gate cavernous opening at the Mountain's foot; source of Running River

thrush large black bird that lives near the mountain

VOCABULARY: Write the meaning of each bold word or phrase.

1. a great **spur** of the mountain n. ridge, edge
2. died away to a **plodding** gloom v. lingering, lumbering
3. **Desolation** of the Dragon n. devastation, ruin
4. the **waning** of the year n. fading, closing
5. alone in the **perilous** waste adj. dangerous, hazardous
6. the dragon's **marauding** feet v. pillaging, raiding
7. they **toiled** in parties v. labored, slaved
8. they **implored** it to move v. begged, entreated

COMPREHENSION QUESTIONS: Answer the following in complete sentences.

1. Why won't the men of the town accompany the dwarves to the Mountain?

   The men aren't sure they believe the dwarves' story is true, and they are afraid of the dragon.

2. What signs indicate that the dragon is still alive and well under the Mountain?

   Smoke, fire, and earthquakes indicate the dragon's well-being.

3. Who unexpectedly finds what they are seeking? Where and what is it?

   Bilbo, Fili, and Kili find the secret door on the side of the Mountain up on a ledge.

4. What methods do the dwarves use to attempt to open the door? Why do you think they are not successful?

They beat on it, push it, implore it to move, and say fragments of broken opening spells. They then use mining methods and tools. It is a magic door, and thus only opens by magic.

5. The dwarves have become dependent on Bilbo's brains and good luck. But have they begun to place blame upon him as well as praise? Summarize the conversation Bilbo overhears.

The dwarves are already blaming Bilbo for not doing what he was hired to do, and thinking of things that he should be doing, such as finding the door.

6. What event causes Bilbo to recall the message in the runes? Explain.

Sitting on the doorstep thinking, Bilbo sees the thrush and hears it knocking snail shells on a rock (Review Chapter 3, "when the thrush knocks ..."), which causes him to recall the message in the runes.

QUOTATIONS

Speaker	Quotation
the men of the town	1. *"Not at any rate until the songs have come true!"*
Balin	2. *"There lies all that is left of Dale."*
Bombur	3. *"I am too fat for such fly-walks. I should turn dizzy and tread on my beard, and then you would be thirteen again."*
Bilbo	4. *"You said sitting on the doorstep and thinking would be my job ..."*

DISCUSSION QUESTIONS

1. What is happening when the second quotation is said?
2. Explain the meaning of this sentence: "They were at the end of their journey, but as far as ever, it seemed, from the end of their quest."
3. What is the importance of this chapter title? Do you remember Bilbo's statement to the dwarves in Chapter 1? In this chapter, what is Bilbo's most important role?

ENRICHMENT

1. Tolkien is not only a great storyteller, he is also a beautiful prose writer. Copy the final paragraph of this chapter in your best penmanship, paying close attention to sentence structure and the mood Tolkien sets with his use of words. Then draw a picture based on the image you conjure up as you read this paragraph.

Chapter 12: Inside Information

"He was in grievous danger of coming under the dragon-spell."

READING NOTES

Arkenstone a great white gem; the heart of the mountain

VOCABULARY: Write the meaning of each bold word or phrase.

1. the others made no **pretence** of offering n. charade, simulation
2. gold **wrought** and unwrought v. formed, shaped
3. **cowered** down in fright. v. shrank, recoiled
4. He **issued** from the Gate v. emerged, came out
5. **replenish** our supplies v. to restock, refill
6. These don't sound so **creditable**. adj. commendable, admirable
7. Your information is **antiquated**. adj. obsolete, old-fashioned
8. his **foreboding** grew n. strong feeling of future misfortune

COMPREHENSION QUESTIONS: Answer the following in complete sentences.

1. What is Bilbo's reaction to Thorin's speech?

   Bilbo is irritated and impatient. He wants to get on with his job. He feels he has already done enough for the dwarves, but now he wants to see the quest through due to his new curiosity and courage.

2. As he sets out for the next phase of the adventure, what does Bilbo now rely upon instead of a pocket-handkerchief?

   Bilbo relies upon his ring, his sword, and his new self-confidence.

3. What is the bravest thing that Bilbo ever does?

   He continues down the tunnel toward Smaug.

4. What is Bilbo's first actual theft? How does this demonstrate the dwarves' unrealistic expectations of their burglar?

A great two-handled cup. The vastness of the treasure would be impossible for Bilbo to carry out an armload at a time; this is no ordinary burglary, and is more than Bilbo could handle alone.

5. How is Bilbo enchanted by the dragon's talk? What does this cause him to suspect?

Smaug seems to be telling the truth about the dwarves, which causes Bilbo to suspect their intention to cheat him out of his reward.

6. What is Bilbo's ploy in discovering Smaug's weak spot?

Bilbo's ploy is to flatter Smaug into showing him his weak spot by calling him "Lord Smaug the Impenetrable" and admiring his waistcoat of diamonds; he knows that Smaug will fall for the flattery and give him a closer look at his belly.

QUOTATIONS

Smaug 1. *"Well, thief! I smell you and I feel your air."*

Bilbo 2. *"Never laugh at live dragons!"*

Thorin 3. *"The Arkenstone! The Arkenstone!"*

Smaug 4. *"They shall see me and remember who is the real King under the Mountain!"*

DISCUSSION QUESTIONS

1. To whom is the first quotation directed?
2. What is the weak point in the dwarves' plans? How does this tie in with the difference between a journey and a quest?
3. The dwarves are anxious to reclaim their treasure. What begins to happen to the dwarves as they near the dragon's hoard?

ENRICHMENT

1. What is the most that could be said about the dwarves? What are their best character traits? Their worst? Add these to your list of dwarfish information.

Chapter 13: Not at Home

"Now I am a burglar indeed!"

VOCABULARY: Write the meaning of each bold word or phrase.

1. **cunning** devilry adj. clever, ingenious
2. a little globe of **pallid** light adj. colorless, ashen
3. a silver-**hafted** axe v. handled, hilted
4. A light helm of **figured** leather v. shaped, crafted
5. the old adornments were long **mouldered** v. disintegrated
6. **furtive** shadows adj. stealthy, secretive
7. fluttering in the **draughts** n. drafts, gusts
8. In all their talk they came **perpetually** back to one thing adv. continually

COMPREHENSION QUESTIONS: Answer the following in complete sentences.

1. What does Bilbo mean by the expression "third time pays for all"?

   Bilbo means that his third time down the tunnel will be successful.

2. While searching the treasure hoard, what does Bilbo find, what does he do, and what does he say about himself?

   He finds the Arkenstone, hides it in his pocket, and withholds it from the dwarves; he calls himself a real burglar.

3. What does the mere glimpse of gold and jewels rekindle in the hearts of the dwarves? Does this urge them on through the cavern?

   It rekindles in the dwarves a fierceness and greed for their rediscovered treasure; yes, this urges them on.

4. What do the dwarves find as they seek a way out of the cavern?

   They find the great chamber of Thror; ancient ruins and relics of their feasts; the source of the Running River.

5. How many days and nights has the Company passed in the darkness of the Mountain?

The Company has passed only two nights and a day, but the darkness has made them lose track of the time.

6. What is "cram"? Who describes it for us? Do we have a modern counterpart?

Cram is biscuitish food, keeps good indefinitely, sustaining but not entertaining, very chewy and tough. The author is giving us an aside to add humor to the description. Hardtack is a modern equivalent.

7. How does Balin know the way out of the Mountain?

Balin is an older dwarf who had once lived under the mountain.

QUOTATIONS

Speaker	Quotation
Bilbo (quoting his father)	1. *"While there's life there's hope!"*
Thorin	2. *"Now what on earth or under it has happened?"*
Balin	3. *"It is about our turn to help, and I am quite willing to go. Anyway I expect it is safe for the moment."*
Bilbo	4. *"I would give a good many of these precious goblets for a drink of something cheering out of one of Beorn's wooden bowls!"*
Thorin	5. *"Don't call my palace a nasty hole! You wait till it has been cleaned and redecorated!"*

DISCUSSION QUESTIONS

1. What is the speaker talking about in the second quotation?
2. Do you have an idea where Smaug is? (Refer to the last paragraph of Chapter 12.) Why is Smaug away? Does the uncertainty of Smaug's whereabouts help to prepare us for what happens next?

ENRICHMENT

1. Read "Inside Information" in the Appendix and complete the "Notes" section.
2. Draw the Arkenstone and copy the description of it under your drawing.

Chapter 14: Fire and Water

"The thought came into his heart of the fabled treasure ... lying without guard or owner."

READING NOTES

Bard a grim man; captain of the archers, descended from Lord Girion of Dale

VOCABULARY: Write the meaning of each bold word or phrase.

1. it was **ominous** and drear adj. alarming, menacing
2. it would **quench** him v. to douse, extinguish
3. **silvered** his great wings v. covered with silver
4. His last **throes** n. struggles, spasms
5. the **waxing** moon v. enlarging, expanding
6. earned an **eminent** place adj. distinguished, prominent
7. For what fault am I to be **deposed**? v. removed from office
8. the Elvenking's **array** n. guard, company

COMPREHENSION QUESTIONS: Answer the following in complete sentences.

1. Who is the only King under the Mountain the townspeople have ever known?

   Smaug

2. Who is the grim-voiced fellow? Why aren't his companions likely to listen to his forebodings? What is his warning to the townspeople?

   Bard; he is often foreboding gloomy things; he warns that the dragon is coming.

3. Why are the townspeople at first fooled by Smaug's coming?

   The lake turns gold with his fire; the townspeople are enthusiastically awaiting the dwarves' successful mission and believe the legends.

4. Why does Smaug intend first to destroy the town rather than seek out and destroy the dwarves?

   Smaug's goal is to prevent the men from coming to the dwarves' aid, and to punish them for playing a part.

5. For what purpose does the Elvenking gather his army to march for the Mountain?

The Elvenking knows the news means war, and he intends to recover his stolen treasure.

6. Where is the new town built? Where does Smaug fall?

The new town is built northward, higher up the shore and away from where the dragon fell. Smaug falls in the lake by the ruins of Lake-town.

QUOTATIONS

a man of Lake-town 1. *"Perhaps the King under the Mountain is forging gold."*

Bard 2. *"The dragon is coming or I am a fool!"*

the thrush 3. *"Look for the hollow of the left breast as he flies and turns above you!"*

the townspeople 4. *"Up the Bowman, and down with Moneybags!"*

Master of the town 5. *"I am the last man to undervalue Bard the Bowman."*

DISCUSSION QUESTIONS

1. How had the information come to light in the third quotation?
2. A company of archers does not give up the fight to defend their town. Bard has spent his last arrow but one, and he is alone. What happens next?
3. In the previous chapter, the dwarves sat outside the Mountain gate wondering about Smaug's absence and noticing the gathering of birds. How is this scene connected with the battle scene in Lake-town? Where are the birds mentioned next? Why did the author write two chapters about the same period of time?

ENRICHMENT

1. Pretend you were a visitor in Esgaroth during Smaug's attack on Lake-town and his ensuing death. Write a letter to someone back home detailing what you have witnessed.

Chapter 15: The Gathering of the Clouds

"Bilbo's heart fell, both at the song and the talk."

READING NOTES

Roac chief of the great ravens of the Mountain; son of Carc

Dain Thorin's cousin and the chief of the dwarves of the Iron Mountains

VOCABULARY: Write the meaning of each bold word or phrase.

1. **carrion** birds adj. feeding on dead flesh
2. a most **decrepit** old bird adj. feeble, frail
3. **caper** about for joy v. to frolic, skip
4. **fortifying** the main entrance v. securing, strengthening
5. there is matter for a **parley** n. conference, meeting
6. the **lust** of it was heavy on him n. longing, yearning
7. evil deeds should be **amended** v. rectified, improved
8. he has **succoured** the people v. aided, helped, assisted

COMPREHENSION QUESTIONS: Answer the following in complete sentences.

1. What indicates to Thorin that something strange is happening?

   The gathering birds indicate something strange.

2. The dwarves are not able to understand the speech of the old thrush. How is his message interpreted to them?

   The thrush understands them and fetches a raven to translate, whose language they do understand.

3. Describe Roac. What is the message he delivers to Thorin?

   He is a large black raven, a decrepit old bird, balding, getting blind; he tells Thorin about the death of Smaug, gathering armies, etc., and gives a warning about the dwarves' treasure.

4. To whom does Thorin ask Roac to send messengers? Why?

Thorin asks Roac to send messengers to his cousin Dain in the Iron Hills; Thorin has decided not to cooperate in giving Bard a share of the treasure and is preparing to do battle.

5. How do the dwarves spend their days awaiting the arrival of the armies?

They fortify the main entrance, find their ponies and supplies, and prepare for a siege.

QUOTATIONS

Roac, son of Carc	1. *"It is a hundred years and three and fifty since I came out of the egg."*
Thorin	2. *"You put your worst cause last and in the chief place."*
messenger of armies	3. *"I declare the Mountain besieged."*
Bilbo	4. *"The whole place still stinks of dragon, and it makes me sick. And cram is beginning simply to stick in my throat."*

DISCUSSION QUESTIONS

1. What is the cause spoken about in the second quotation?
2. Read the dwarves' song. Go back to the first song. Combine the two. Do they tell a complete story? Which verse(s) of the second song are almost identical to the first? Now that the foe in the first song is dead, what foe is referred to in the new song?
3. Do you think Bard's request for one-twelfth portion of the treasure is reasonable? Why does Thorin reject his claim? What do you think of Thorin and the dwarves? Is their behavior typical of human nature? Do you think their selfish cause will succeed? Explain.
4. Why do you think the author ends this chapter with Bilbo's discontented thoughts? Try to guess what happens next. (See the title of the next chapter for a clue.)

ENRICHMENT

1. Memorize the dwarves' song from this chapter, and recite it to your class.

Chapter 16: A Thief in the Night

"A hobbit in elvish armour ... was something new to them."

READING NOTES

Dwarf and Goblin Wars seven-year war in which dwarves hunted goblins of the North

VOCABULARY: Write the meaning of each bold word or phrase.

1. I will be **avenged** v. vindicated, justified
2. an old bundle of tattered **oddments** n. scraps, leftovers
3. **grievous** to bear adj. grave, severe
4. so far past our **sentinels** n. guards, sentries
5. looked more **comely** in it adj. attractive, handsome
6. here you shall be honoured and **thrice** welcome adv. three times
7. an **escort** was provided n. guide, attendant
8. There is news **brewing** v. stirring, looming

COMPREHENSION QUESTIONS: Answer the following in complete sentences.

1. What is Bilbo's plan that is revealed at the beginning of Chapter 16?
   Bilbo tries to make peace by giving the Arkenstone to Bard.
2. Thorin is obsessed with finding the Arkenstone. Where does Bilbo have it concealed?
   Bilbo has the Arkenstone wrapped in rags, and he is using it as a pillow.
3. Do you think it is fortunate that Bombur is on night watch? Why?
   Yes. Bombur has been sleepy since his enchantment in Mirkwood and is easily convinced by Bilbo to leave the watch.
4. Bilbo is well received into the "enemy" camp, but both armies are not willing to make peace. Why not? What changes the discussion?
   Pride on both sides and distrust of one another keep the armies from a willingness to make peace. Bilbo's offer of the Arkenstone changes the discussion.

QUOTATIONS

Thorin 1. *"For the Arkenstone of my father is worth more than a river of gold in itself, and to me it is beyond price."*

Bombur 2. *"Not that I venture to disagree with Thorin, may his beard grow ever longer; yet he was ever a dwarf with a stiff neck."*

Bilbo 3. *"I would give a good deal for the feel of grass at my toes."*

Bilbo 4. *"I have an interest in this matter—one fourteenth share, to be precise ..."*

Gandalf 5. *"Well done! Mr. Baggins! There is always more about you than anyone expects!"*

DISCUSSION QUESTIONS

1. What effect upon Bilbo does the first quotation have?
2. Why do you think Gandalf is pleased with Bilbo's plan? Is this another allusion to "predestination" or Providence? Bilbo chooses to do this of his own free will, yet Gandalf has been hoping this would be his choice. How does this interplay reveal Gandalf's position as prophet/angel?

ENRICHMENT

1. When Bilbo first set out on this adventure, he had no desire for treasure; he longed for the simple comforts of home. When he encountered the dwarves' treasure hoard, he was influenced with the desire of dwarves. Now he willingly gives up the dwarves' greatest treasure in order to end the battle and return to the comforts of home (after giving away the Arkenstone, he dreams of bacon and eggs). Did it ever appear that Bilbo would change? Write a short essay on this theme.

Answers will vary, but should point out that Bilbo's ability to do grand and brave deeds does not negate his love of simple life. Instead, it serves to protect the values he holds dear: home, peace, friendship, etc.

Chapter 17: The Clouds Burst

"So began a battle that none had expected."

READING NOTES

Bolg of the North Goblin ruler whose father Dain had killed in the Goblin Wars

Battle of Five Armies a battle of goblins and wargs against elves, men, and dwarves

VOCABULARY: Write the meaning of each bold word or phrase.

1. I could not **forbear** to redeem v. to refrain, abstain
2. **hauberk** of steel mail n. a long defensive shirt extending to the knees
3. Their beards were forked and **plaited** and thrust into their belts. v. braided, tressed
4. upon their right **flank** n. side, wing
5. bring **reconciliation** n. resolution, compromise
6. the **vanguard** swirled round the spur's end n. front, advancement
7. a **feint** of resistance n. a fake move, ploy, ruse
8. stemmed the first **onslaught** n. attack, blitz

COMPREHENSION QUESTIONS: Answer the following in complete sentences.

1. Is it a good thing Gandalf appears for the final adventure? What is his part?

   It is a good thing because he saves Bilbo, prevents the war, and diverts the attention to the new danger.

2. What is the Elvenking's attitude?

   The Elvenking does not want to fight a war over gold.

3. What is Thorin's decision after that last meeting with Bard?

   He sends word to Dain to hurry and to continue with the siege until more help arrives, and not to give in.

4. Why do the dwarves, men, and elves suddenly decide they are no longer enemies?

They realize the need to unite against the goblins, who are the more dreaded common enemy.

5. Does Bilbo doubt their victory? Why or why not? What is the turning point of the battle?

Yes, Bilbo doubts their victory because the goblins keep coming and are cutting off the armies; the arrival of the eagles is the turning point.

6. Why do you think Thorin changes his mind about giving a portion of the treasure to Bard?

Thorin calculates that the coming of winter will stop the siege. Also, his greed is driving him, and the possibility of winning due to the approach of Dain and reinforcements.

QUOTATIONS

Thorin 1. *"My mind does not change with the rising and setting of a few suns."*

Gandalf 2. *"If you don't like my Burglar, please don't damage him."*

Thorin 3. *"You all seem in league! What have you to say, you descendant of rats?"*

Bilbo 4. *"Is this all the service of you and your family that I was promised?"*

Elvenking 5. *"Long will I tarry, ere I begin this war for gold."*

Bilbo 6. *"The Eagles are coming!"*

DISCUSSION QUESTIONS

1. Who is the "descendant of rats" spoken to in the third quotation?
2. In the last chapter, we discussed Bilbo's choice to give up his share of the treasure. Now we are seeing Thorin's side of things. Thorin accuses Bilbo of being a burglar, but that was his job description from the beginning. Discuss the irony of this accusation. What causes Thorin to turn against Bilbo? What causes Bilbo to do what he does?

ENRICHMENT

1. Read aloud the descriptive passage of Thorin's dramatic entry into the war with his army. Then draw a picture of Thorin in his battle attire as he enters the fray. Write his call-to-war under your picture.

Chapter 18: The Return Journey

"He wept until his eyes were red and his voice was hoarse."

VOCABULARY: Write the meaning of each bold word or phrase.

1. the goblins' **mustering** v. assembling, gathering
2. bore him out of the **fray** n. conflict, skirmish
3. his wrath was **redoubled** v. intensified, renewed
4. the **trackless** dark adj. unmarked
5. Victory had been **assured** v. secured, guaranteed
6. **Yule-tide** was warm n. Christmas

COMPREHENSION QUESTIONS: Answer the following in complete sentences.

1. Who is waiting to say farewell to Bilbo? How does their meeting end?

   Thorin; he is dying and wants to apologize to Bilbo and thank him for his help. Bilbo weeps, and they part in kindness.

2. Who buries Thorin? What is placed on his breast? Is this a good idea?

   Bard buries Thorin; the Arkenstone is placed on his breast; yes—the King under the Mountain has his treasure.

3. Who places what upon Thorin's tomb?

   The Elvenking places Orcrist, the elvish sword, upon the tomb.

4. Which dwarves have fallen in battle? How many now remain?

   Fili and Kili fell in battle, leaving ten remaining dwarves.

5. Who becomes king in Thorin's place? Is he a better king? Why or why not?

   Dain becomes king; he is a better king because he is not greedy.

6. What does Bilbo give to the Elvenking? What is his reason?

Bilbo gives the necklace of silver and pearls to the Elvenking to repay the king for his invisible burglary.

7. What treasure does Bilbo carry with him?

Bilbo carries a chest of silver and a chest of gold, laden on a pony.

8. Who begins the journey home with Bilbo? Who do they stop to visit on the way?

Bilbo, Gandalf, and Beorn begin their journey with the Elvenking and his army; they spend the winter with Beorn.

9. What happens to Bilbo? Is this good or bad, or both?

Bilbo is knocked unconscious by a rock; this is both good and bad: the enemy doesn't notice and kill him, but he is left outside all night because he is invisible.

QUOTATIONS

Bilbo	1. *"This invisibility has its drawbacks after all."*
Thorin	2. *"There is more in you of good than you know, child of the kindly West."*
Bard	3. *"There let it lie till the Mountain falls!"*
Elvenking	4. *"Farewell! O Gandalf! May you ever appear where you are most needed and least expected!"*

DISCUSSION QUESTIONS

1. What are the drawbacks of invisibility mentioned in the first quotation?

ENRICHMENT

1. As Bilbo's adventure comes to a close, summarize the lessons he has learned. What has he learned about dwarves? About elves? Is he wiser for his experiences? What does he now value? Has this changed? Is he now richer in character than in gold? Summarize Bilbo's reflections in a short essay.

Dwarves - good people, but too easily influenced by gold. Elves - good people, but too suspicious of others. Bilbo is wiser. He has learned how wide the world is, and his experiences with other people have taught him to value their interests. He has learned that he is gifted with abilities that he never knew he had: bravery, wisdom, leadership, selflessness. He is richer in many ways, but most of all in his own understanding of himself and the world.

Chapter 19: The Last Stage

"You are only quite a little fellow in a wide world after all!"

VOCABULARY: Write the meaning of each bold word or phrase.

1. **brink** of the valley n. threshold, edge
2. lower **glades** of the wood n. hollows, clearings
3. masters of **lore** n. wisdom, tradition, knowledge
4. Sale to **commence** at ten o'clock sharp v. to begin, start
5. **Presumed** Dead v. supposed
6. a great deal more than a **nine days' wonder** n. something famous a short time
7. Mr. Baggins' waistcoat was more **extensive** adj. broad, vast
8. Lake-town was **refounded** v. rebuilt, reestablished

COMPREHENSION QUESTIONS: Answer the following in complete sentences.

1. What business had occupied Gandalf while the Company was on its quest?

   He and the council of the white wizards had driven the evil Necromancer out of Mirkwood.

2. What do Bilbo and Gandalf find when they come to the place where they encountered the trolls? What does Gandalf insist, and why?

   They find the gold of the trolls, which they had buried a year ago. Gandalf insists that Bilbo keep some of the gold because he may find more need of it than he expects—perhaps for another adventure?

3. Where does Bilbo finally get a pocket-handkerchief? What meaning do you think the author intended for this little detail in the story?

   Elrond has given him a red silk hankie; Bilbo is now returning to his comfortable life, where handkerchiefs are necessary.

4. What does Bilbo do to make Gandalf wonder what is the matter with him?

   He bursts into song when he sees the panorama of his homeland; his year with elves and dwarves has given him the habit of singing.

5. How does Bilbo's adventure change his habits and personality?

Bilbo is labeled as "queer," but he does not care; he is content. He spends his gold and silver on presents, keeps his magic ring a secret, and takes to writing poetry and visiting elves.

6. Who pays Bilbo an unexpected visit? From what you have gathered in the story, why does this particular dwarf come to see Bilbo? What news does he bring of Dale?

Gandalf and Balin; Balin is the dwarf most fond of Bilbo. Balin tells how Bard has rebuilt the town in Dale and made the rivers run with gold. Lake-town has been refounded. The Master of the town has come to a bad end.

QUOTATIONS

Bilbo 1. *"Your lullaby would waken a drunken goblin!"*

elves of Rivendell 2. *"And your snores would waken a stone dragon."*

Gandalf 3. *"My dear Bilbo! Something is the matter with you! You are not the hobbit that you were."*

DISCUSSION QUESTIONS

1. Throughout his journeys, Bilbo keeps the end in view: comfort and home. In your opinion, what would have happened to Bilbo had he arrived at Bag-End a few days too late?

ENRICHMENT

1. What are Gandalf's final remarks to Bilbo? How does this last conversation sum up Bilbo's experiences? Write a summary of the journey from Bilbo's viewpoint of "there and back again."
2. If you know the story of *The Odyssey*, write a comparison between these two stories.

1. Gandalf reminds Bilbo that his adventures and fortunes do not happen simply by luck. By calling Bilbo quite a little fellow in a wide world, Gandalf points to the fact that there is a greater power at work, guiding the fates of people in the world. The conversation sums up Bilbo's experience in terms of divine sovereignty, or the work of God in the world to bring all things under His purpose. Bilbo's viewpoint of "there and back again" summarizes his journey by dividing it into two places: "there" refers to the lands of the adventure, and "back again" refers to Bilbo's home. For Bilbo, the journey was always about this division; if he was weary of the adventure, it was because he missed home, and if he endured and pressed on to fulfill the adventure, it was so that he could return home the sooner.

2. The stories are alike in a few ways. Odysseus and Bilbo both go on adventures where they meet monsters and magical creatures. They both desire to return home, and when they do, they find their possessions being divided among others in the town. Each character's journey involves war against an enemy who has stolen something valuable. Each uses cleverness and wisdom in their adventure.

APPENDIX

Book Notes: Dwarves

Start a list of the 13 dwarves and record their appearance as described in each chapter. As you read the book, add additional information about their personality traits and special skills. Number the dwarves as their names appear in the text.

1. Dwalin: blue beard tucked into golden belt, dark green hood

2. Balin: odd-looking, white beard, scarlet hood, look-out man, most fond of and loyal to Bilbo

3. & 4. Fili and Kili: blue hoods, silver belts, yellow beards, bags of tools and spades, sharp eyes, used as scouts because they are the youngest pair of dwarves

5. Dori: purple hood, carried Bilbo on his back and helped him climb the tree in Mirkwood, shared Bilbo's views about meals (regular and often)

6. Nori: purple hood (similar to Dori)

7. Ori: gray hood

8. Oin: brown hood, both Oin and Gloin are good at making fires, fight together often

9. Gloin: white hood; questions Bilbo's abilities as a burglar

10. & 11. Bifor and Bofur: yellow hoods

12. Bombur: pale green hood, fat, fell into enchanted stream at Mirkwood and loved to sleep ever afterward; was look-out guard the night Bilbo went to the enemy camp in "Thief in the Night"

13. Thorin: sky-blue hood with silver tassel, King under the Mountain, leader of Company, loves to make pompous speeches, rather grumpy but kind and generous; loved the Arkenstone; dies in battle, very courageous but snared by greed and pride of the dragon hoard

Book Notes: Characters

Students can fill in the Book Notes from the Reading Notes for each lesson. Answers will vary. Major characters to include would be Bilbo Baggins, Gandalf, Thorin, Smaug, The Great Goblin, Gollum, Beorn, The Elvenking, Bard, etc.

Bilbo Baggins: well-to-do hobbit living at The Hill in Hobbiton

Gandalf: wizard who knew Bilbo's grandfather, the Old Took

Thorin: important dwarf leading a band of twelve other dwarves

Smaug: dragon who stole the dwarves' home and treasure

The Great Goblin: the ruler of the goblins under the Misty Mountains

Gollum: a small slimy wicked creature living by the lake down beneath the mountain

Beorn: a good man living near Mirkwood who transforms into a bear

The Elvenking: the king of the Wood-elves of Mirkwood; good but stern

Bard: a grim man; captain of the archers, descended from Lord Girion of Dale

Book Notes: Creature List

Start a list of the different races/creatures encountered in *The Hobbit*. Describe each race or creature, giving appearance, personality, activities, homeland, etc.

1. Hobbits ____

____

____

____

____

2. Dwarves ____

____

____

____

____

3. Wizards ____

____

____

____

____

4. Elves ____

____

____

____

____

5. Trolls ____

____

____

____

____

Book Notes: Places

Students can fill in the Book Notes from the Reading Notes for each lesson. Answers will vary. Major places to include would be Hobbiton, Lonely Mountain, Rivendell, Misty Mountains, Mirkwood, Dale, Lake-town, etc.

Hobbiton: Bilbo's hometown

Lonely Mountain: mountain where Smaug lives, hoarding the dwarves' treasure; originally the home of Thorin and his kin

Rivendell: place where Elrond lives in the Last Homely House; where the Company stops after their encounter with the trolls

Misty Mountains: mountain range under which the goblins and Gollum live

Mirkwood: a terrible forest; the last peril before the Lonely Mountain

Dale: once-thriving town of men near the Lonely Mountain

Lake-town: town of men on the surface of the Long Lake

Book Notes: Adventures

Students should list each of Bilbo's adventures on this page as they come across them in their reading. Start with the invasion of the dwarves into Bilbo's hobbit hole and go from there. Answers will vary.

Book Notes: Summaries

This page can be used to complete the summary assignments in the Enrichment section of Chapter 1 (history of the dwarves) and in the Enrichment section of Chapter 19 (summary of Bilbo's journey). Answers will vary.

Spelling / Usage

SPELLING

1. further/farther "farther" denotes physical distance; only "further" is adj. or adverb
2. hither/thither "hither" is to or toward here; "thither" is away from here
3. Learn these spelling demons: handkerchief, suffocated, gorgeous
4. Homophones: horde/hoard
5. Homonyms: row/row
6. Masonry terms: joint, crevice, post, lintel, threshold, bar, bolt, keyhole

Note this: dwarf / dwarves

GIVE THE AMERICAN SPELLINGS OF THESE BRITISH WORDS:

1. clamour clamor
2. cosily cozily
3. grey gray
4. armour armor
5. traveller traveler
6. neighbour neighbor
7. splendour splendor
8. parlour parlor
9. councillor counselor
10. honour honor
11. marvellous marvelous
12. humour humor
13. colour color
14. favourite favorite
15. valour valor
16. carcasse carcass

GIVE MEANINGS FOR THESE ARCHAIC WORDS:

1. breeches pants
2. benighted overtaken by night
3. waistcoat vest
4. portcullis grate
5. chestnut old, repeated story or joke
6. fretted worried
7. oddments parts, fragments
8. furrier a fur dealer
9. unbeknown not known
10. mead beer made of honey
11. bracken large fern
12. hart male deer
13. shirking putting off
14. champing biting or grinding
15. fetch retrieve, get
16. smote hit
17. larch a kind of tree
18. flagons large cups
19. dell valley
20. quaff drink
21. turnkey prison guard
22. bidding wish, desire
23. hewn cut, chopped
24. plight trouble
25. quest a journey with a goal
26. fell a stony hill
27. lade burdened, loaded
28. hark listen
29. realm large area, country
30. dratted confounded
31. fortnight two weeks
32. throve / thriven grow

TOLKIEN WORDS:

gnawingly hungry
hooting and hallooing
bebother
parchingly thirsty
confusticate
miserableness / miserabler

Runic Alphabet

Figure out the Runic Alphabet by using Thror's map, Gandalf's translation of the runes in Chapter 1, and Elrond's translation in Chapter 3.

F

U/V

TH

O/OO

R

Z

C

K

G

W

H

N

I/J

X

S

T

B

E

M

L

NG

D

A

EE

Y

EA

NOTE: The runes for "U" and "I" are used for "V" and "J."

Runic Alphabet Translation

Translate the following two runic sentences:

1. ᚦᛖ·ᚻᚩᛒᛒᛁᛏ·ᚩᚱ·ᚦᛖᚱᛖ·ᚪᚾᛞ·ᛒᚪᚳᚳ·ᚪᚷᚪᛁᚾ·ᛒᛖᛁᛝ·ᚦᛖ·ᚱᛖᚳᚩᚱᛞᛋ·
ᚩᚠ·ᚪ·ᛠᚱᛋ·ᛄᚩᚢᚱᚾᛖᛠ·ᛗᚪᛞᛖ·ᛒᛠ·ᛒᛁᛚᛒᚩ·ᛒᚪᚷᚷᛁᚾᛋ·ᚩᚠ·ᚻᚩᛒᛒᛁᛏᚩᚾ:

The Hobbit or There and Back Again Being the Records of a Years Journey Made by Bilbo Baggins of Hobbiton.

2. ᚳᚩᛗᛈᛁᛚᛖᛞ·ᚠᚱᚩᛗ·ᚻᛁᛋ·ᛗᛖᛗᚩᛁᚱᛋ·ᛒᛠ·ᛁᚱᚱ·ᛏᚩᛚᚳᛁᛖᚾ·ᚪᚾᛞ·
ᛈᚢᛒᛚᛁᛋᚻᛖᛞ·ᛒᛠ·ᚷᛖᚩᚱᚷᛖ·ᚪᛚᛚᛖᚾ·ᚪᚾᛞ·ᚢᚾᚹᛁᚾ·ᛚᛏᛗ:

Compiled from His Memoirs by J. R. R. Tolkien and Published by George Allen and Unwin LTM.

Translate these inscriptions on Thror's map:

3. ᚠᛁᚢᛖ·ᚠᛟᛏ·ᚻᛁᚷᚻ·ᚦᛖ·ᛞᚩᚱ·ᚪᚾᛞ·ᚦᚱᛟ·ᛗᚪᛠ·ᚹᚪᛚᚳ·ᚪᛒᚱᛖᚪᛋᛏ:ᚦᚦ

Five feet high the door and three may walk abreast. TH.TH.

4. ᛋᛏᚪᚾᛞ·ᛒᛠ·ᚦᛖ·ᚷᚱᛖᛠ·ᛋᛏᚩᚾᛖ·ᚻᚹᛖᚾ·ᚦᛖ·ᚦᚱᚢᛋᚻ·ᚳᚾᚩᚳᚳᛋ·ᚪᚾᛞ·
ᚦᛖ·ᛋᛖᛏᛏᛁᛝ·ᛋᚢᚾ·ᚹᛁᚦ·ᚦᛖ·ᛚᚪᛋᛏ·ᛚᛁᚷᚻᛏ·ᚩᚠ·ᛞᚢᚱᛁᚾᛋ·ᛞᚪᛠ·ᚹᛁᛚᛚ·
ᛋᚻᛁᚾᛖ·ᚢᛈᚩᚾ·ᚦᛖ·ᚳᛖᛠᚻᚩᛚᛖ:

Stand by the grey stone hwen (when) the thrush knocks and the setting sun with the last light of Durin's Day will shine upon the keyhole.

The Story Behind a Name

The author of *The Hobbit*, J. R. R. Tolkien, thought that there was more to a name than just a random combination of letters. A name has a meaning; it refers to something else. For example, when you hear or read the word *dwarf*, a picture comes into your mind. Your picture may be a little different than someone else's (e.g., a short, stout man with a long beard and stocking cap), but it is nevertheless a concept you have gotten and stored in your head. Words have meaning because they point to something we have come to know by discovering in everyday life. Of course, you have probably never seen a dwarf in person, and dwarves are not "real," in a sense, because you cannot go up to one and shake his hand. On the other hand, you know what a dwarf is because there are stories about them. The word *dwarf* means something to us because dwarves have a story—in fact, many stories. You are in the midst of reading one now, and there are other stories about dwarves you have read before or might read in the future (e.g., *Snow White and the Seven Dwarves*). Stories are what give meaning to a name like *dwarf* beyond just the sound that the letters d-w-a-r-f make when said together. In summary, a name has meaning because there's a story behind it.

One day Tolkien was reading a very old book called the *Poetic Edda*, and he came across a list of names. Although the list said little about who the people were, Tolkien knew that they must have had some meaning and significance, or else the author would not have included them. As he was pondering these names, he started to guess at the stories behind them. Take a look at the list yourself, and see what you think he came up with:

Mótsognir rose, mightiest ruler
of the kin of dwarfs, but Durin was another;
They molded many manlike bodies
—the dwarfs under earth, as Durin said.

Nýi and Nithi, 2 Northri and Suthri,
Austri and Vestri, 3 Althjóf, Dwalin,
Nár and Náin, Níping, Dáin,
Bifur, Bofur, Bombur, Nóri,
Án and Onar, Ái, Mjóthvitnir.

Veig and Gandálf, Vindálf, Thráin,
Thekk and Thorin, Thrór, Vit, and Lit,
Nár and Regin, Nýráth and Ráthsvith;
now is reckoned the roster of dwarfs.

Two dwarves from an edition of Völuspá (1895), by Lorenz Frølich

You probably recognized a few names: Dwalin, Bifur, Bofur, Bombur, Nori, Thorin, Durin (the ancestor of the dwarves), and Gandalf. As Tolkien pondered these names, he was puzzled by this last one. The last part of Gandalf, "alf," is another spelling for "elf." Tolkien knew that elves were always kept distinct from dwarves in old myths and tales. He also knew that the first part of the name, "Gand," meant "wand" or "wizard's staff." Tolkien concluded that the name "Gandalf," or "staff-elf," must have belonged to an elf-like person with magical powers, indeed, a wizard. If that was the case, asked Tolkien, then what was a wizard doing in a list of dwarves? Could it be that long ago a band of dwarves had gotten mixed in with a wizard on some adventure? That is, at least, the story Tolkien saw behind the names.

The Story of Your Name

Your name has a story behind it. It has a meaning, a history, and it sums up a lot of information in just a few letters. When you introduce yourself to someone by giving your name, from then on that person will attach your name to a particular human being, who is different from every other human being, and who plays a unique part in the world. Your name, therefore, is important, because it's a summary of you. Answer the questions below to better understand the story of your name.

EXERCISE 1: What does your name mean to others who know you? Go to someone who has known you your whole life, such as a parent, and ask them to answer the following questions about your name:

1. How was my name chosen?

____

____

____

2. What does my name mean?

____

____

____

EXERCISE 2: Imagine that you were a person living in Middle-Earth, the ancient world where *The Hobbit* takes place. Then imagine that J. R. R. Tolkien came across your name in some old book and decided to write a story in which you were one of the characters. He would have certain questions about you, like what kind of being you were and what adventures you undertook. Answer the following questions that he might have asked when he came across your name.

1. What race is this person (e.g., dwarf, elf, wizard, hobbit, etc.)?

____

____

____

2. What part of Middle-Earth do they come from (e.g., Hobbiton, Mirkwood, the Misty Mountains, etc.)?

____

3. What adventure were they involved in?

____

____

____

____

____

Inside Information

Have you ever watched a movie that reminded you of another story or movie? There may have been a scene or character that looked like one from another story. When one story makes an unannounced reference to another story, it is called an allusion.[1] The author will not say that he or she is alluding to something else when doing it; the reader is expected to see it without being told directly that it is there. One recent and popular example is the movie *Shrek*. There are dozens of allusions to other stories throughout this animated film. At the end of the movie, for instance, Gingy the gingerbread man says, "God bless us, everyone." If you had read or seen a version of Charles Dickens' *A Christmas Carol* before seeing this movie, when you heard this quote you would have been reminded of the little boy named Tiny Tim, who says the very same line at the end of Dickens' story. Allusions, therefore, are like echoes. An echo is not the same thing as the sound that it came from, since it is softer and less clear, but it is similar enough to the first sound to be recognized as coming from it. And so it is with allusions. The gingerbread man is not the exact same person as Tiny Tim, but they have some similarities and they say the exact same line. An allusion is not the same thing as the source from which it comes, but is recognizable to a reader who knows the source.

Tiny Tim and Bob Cratchit as depicted in the 1870s by Fred Barnard

Of course, in order to recognize an allusion, a reader has to have read its source. Remember, allusions are not spelled out for the reader. The reader is expected to already have "inside information" about the source being echoed. Many readers, including you and me, miss allusions all the time because we don't recognize their source. Just as an inside joke is not funny to those without the background knowledge, so an allusion goes over the heads of readers without prior knowledge of its source. Yet, if you have that prior knowledge, or inside information, allusions can give you a fuller, richer, and more enjoyable experience when reading. Many scenes from *Shrek* are funny to a young child because of their silly antics and fairy tale qualities, but they are even funnier to an older person who recognizes the humorous allusions they make. The reason for this is not because you have to be an adult to enjoy allusions, but that you have to be informed. The best way to be informed is to develop and grow a love for reading.

Let us practice by reading a bit from a story written long ago in England called *Beowulf*. This is a story about knights, monsters, a dragon, and especially the hero named Beowulf. It is quite an adventure, and it's a story you will do well to read in full in later years. It is such an old tale that it has become a source for many allusions in newer stories.

As you read the section below, ask what story or scene from a story may be echoing this source.

> And so it was that the kingship of that broad land came into Beowulf's hands, and he ruled it well for fifty winters. He was a venerable old king who protected his land, until on dark nights, one dragon began to rage. It guarded a hoard high upon a hill in a steep barrow of stone. A straight path led beneath the hill; it was seldom traveled by men. One man, however, chanced upon that cave and saw the heathen's hoard. While the watcher slept, he took in his hand a golden goblet and did not give it back. The guardian's wrath would soon make the prince and people pay for

A 1908 depiction of Beowulf fighting the unnamed dragon, by J. R. Skelton

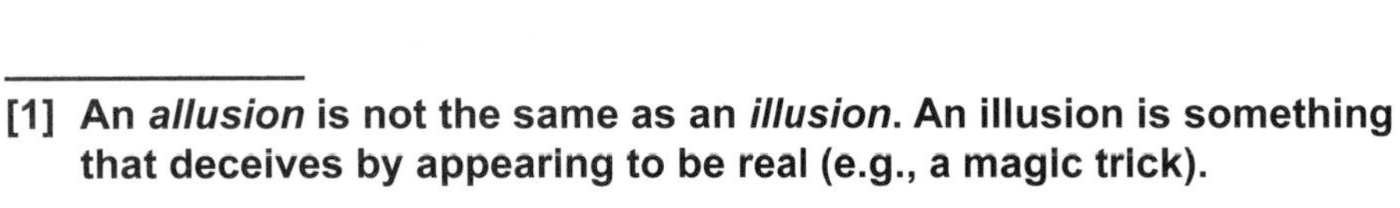

[1] An *allusion* is not the same as an *illusion*. An illusion is something that deceives by appearing to be real (e.g., a magic trick).

> those thievish wiles! … When the dragon awoke, this new quarrel was kindled. He immediately sniffed the scent of the stone. The dark-hearted one found the footprints of that foe who had walked undetected by the creature's head … The guardian of gold went tracking over the ground, eager to find the man who had brought mischief upon his slumber. Savage and burning, he circled 'round the barrow; no man was in that wasteland. Yet he desired war and was eager for combat. He entered and sought the cup, soon discovering that a mortal had sifted through his treasure, the noble gold.

Did you notice anything familiar? Perhaps a few words rung a bell: *dragon, hoard, golden goblet/cup, thief, undetected, slumber, wasteland*. Think about these words and explain the ways that J. R. R. Tolkien alludes to this story in *The Hobbit*. You may discuss what you discover with someone else, and you may record what you find on the lines below.

NOTES:

DISCUSSION QUESTIONS ANSWER KEY

Discussion Questions Answer Key

Chapter 1

1. Explain why the second and fourth quotations show us two different sides of the speaker.
   The second quotation shows Bilbo's plain and comfort-loving side, but the fourth quotation shows that he also has a yearning for adventure.

2. From where have the dwarves come? Why did they move south?
   They were driven from their homes in the far North. Thorin's ancestor, Thrain the Old, had discovered the Mountain and the treasure, and they moved in order to establish a kingdom under the Mountain.

3. Describe the glory days of the dwarves and their relationship with the men of Dale.
   The dwarves improved the Mountain and made it a great kingdom, and Thror was called the King under the Mountain. The men of Dale traded food and goods in exchange for the beautiful things the dwarves crafted, and they paid the dwarves well. They wanted their sons to be apprenticed by the dwarves.

4. Explain the decline in the work and prestige of the dwarves as they changed from craftsmen to blacksmiths to coal miners.
   When Smaug destroyed their kingdom, they were scattered across the land. They were then forced to use their great skills for their plain and degrading jobs as blacksmiths and coal miners.

Chapter 2

1. Describe what is happening in the drawing in this chapter.
   A dwarf is approaching the trolls' campfire, while they lurk behind the fire among the trees.

2. Is Bilbo an optimist or a pessimist? Find specific phrases to support your answer.
   Pessimist: "Bother burgling and everything to do with it!"

3. Compare Thorin's and Gandalf's attempts at rescuing the dwarves. Who is successful? Why?
   Gandalf is successful by exploiting the natural characteristics of trolls (know your enemy) rather than by confrontation, which was Thorin's unsuccessful tactic.

4. Bilbo is hired as a burglar. What are some hobbit characteristics that fit the job description?
   Quiet, sizes up the situation, keeps his wits, etc.

Chapter 3

1. In the third quotation, where is the speaker when he says this?
   Bilbo says it as they approach Elrond's house in Rivendell.

2. The adventure with the trolls is not an accident. What does the Company find in the trolls' lair? Where did the swords come from? How does Elrond know? Is this a foreboding that they are on the right road to their quest?
   The swords found in the lair came from Gondolin of the High Elves of the West. Elrond knows because he is an elf of ancient ancestry. The swords' discovery is a good foreboding.

Chapter 4

1. Describe the drawing in this chapter entitled "The Mountain Path."
   The mountain path is treacherously set among jagged cliffs, and lightning fills the air.

2. The first paragraph of this chapter is a metaphor about any adventure or quest in one's life. Explain.
   There are many paths to take in life, and many will lead to danger and bad ends.

3. "And that was the last time that they used the ponies, packages, baggages, tools and paraphernalia that they had brought with them." To what does this sentence allude? Would they find provisions for the rest of the journey? Explain.
   The goblins' capture of the Company makes the reader wonder what's ahead, and hope that this is not the end of the story, for they would have use for other things ... See goblin song.

4. Goblins are clever but not creative. What is the purpose of their inventions?
   They make tunnels, but they are dirty and untidy. They like explosions and invent tools for torture. They never make beautiful things like the dwarves. They sing only coarse, cruel songs.

Chapter 5

1. What is the speaker talking about in the second quotation?
   Bilbo

2. In narrative form, tell about Bilbo's discovery of the ring, his encounter with Gollum, and his escape.
   Answers will vary.

Chapter 6

1. Describe what is shown in the drawing located in this chapter, and tell where a person would be standing if they were seeing this view.
   It is a view of the Misty Mountains looking west from the eagles' eyrie towards the Goblin Gate. An eagle is in flight over the eyrie, and the Goblin Gate is shown as a shaded spot beneath the smaller peaks at the upper right. A person seeing this view would be standing to the east of the eyrie and west of the Great River.

2. What about Bilbo is the speaker referring to in the first quotation?
   Gandalf knows that Bilbo must have had some special help escaping and getting past Balin.

3. Bilbo thinks he has left the dwarves under the mountains; the dwarves think that Bilbo has been left behind. Compare their different reactions to the thought of returning to the goblins' stronghold to search for their lost companions.
   Bilbo feels responsible for his friends, and has determined to go back for them. The dwarves do not think it is worth going back for Bilbo.

4. How does Gandalf settle the issue?
   He says that either the dwarves go back with him to get Bilbo or he will leave them to fend for themselves.

5. Why does Bilbo keep his ring a secret from the dwarves and Gandalf?
   Bilbo perhaps wants the dwarves to respect him and not dismiss his success on the ring.

Chapter 7

1. Describe what is pictured in the drawing entitled "Beorn's Hall."
   It is a long and high hall with two parallel rows of pillars supporting the roof and running the length of the hall. In the center is a fire pit ablaze, sending smoke through an opening in the roof. In the foreground is a long table with stumps as chairs on both sides.

2. In the third quotation, what is the speaker talking about?
   The dwarves.

3. Retell Gandalf's trick of introducing the dwarves to Beorn, two by two. What is Beorn's reaction? How did he practice this same trick with Bilbo in Chapter 1? Compare the two incidents.
   Instead of all coming at once, Gandalf has the dwarves come two by two, so as not to surprise Beorn and make him angry. It works, and Beorn becomes more and more interested in their story with each new pair. Gandalf did the same to Bilbo, but sent a little more each time. He did it to not overwhelm Bilbo, so as to better coax him into joining the adventure, while with Beorn he is concerned about his temper.

4. Describe the area where Beorn lives, and contrast it to Mirkwood forest.
   Beorn's area is an oak wood with patches of flowers, honeybees, and a high thorn-hedge surrounding his house. Mirkwood, however, is a dense, dark, and terrible forest, where there is little food and water.

Chapter 8

1. What is the speaker talking about in the last quotation, and why does he give it this name?
   Bilbo is talking about his elvish dagger, which he calls "Sting" because the spiders say it is a sting.

2. Describe the change that comes over Bilbo after his encounter with the spiders. Do you think this would have happened without the ring? Is this why Gandalf told the dwarves that Bilbo could be trusted to take care of them? Is it really the ring or is it Bilbo? Explain.
   Bilbo is even more respected by the dwarves, and he proves Gandalf's assumptions correct. The ring helps Bilbo, but it is his courage and loyalty that make the biggest difference.

3. Because the Wood-elves elude and later capture the dwarves, they appear to be hostile. Using the description found in the chapter, summarize the characteristics of this race.
   They are not wicked, but overly distrustful of strangers. They have strong magic, but are more dangerous and less wise than the High Elves of the West. All in all, they are good.

Chapter 9

1. What plan of Bilbo's is referred to in the last quotation?
   The plan is for Bilbo to close up the dwarves into barrels to be sent down the river out of the Elvenking's halls.

2. Why does Gandalf leave the Company to fend for themselves? Is Bilbo living up to Gandalf's expectations? Combine information from the previous chapter with the allusions given in this chapter.
   Gandalf has other business down South. Bilbo is doing as Gandalf said, proving to be invaluable to the dwarves. In the previous chapter, just before leaving the party, Gandalf had said, only half-jokingly, to Bilbo, "You have got to look after all these dwarves for me." It turns out that's exactly what he does, as Gandalf knew.

Chapter 10

1. Describe the details pictured in the drawing of "Lake Town."
   The foreground shows a man on a raft collecting barrels. A shore is on the left side, and the Long Lake takes up the rest of the picture, with Lake-town in the middle.

2. In the first quotation, to whom is Bilbo speaking, and why does he ask this question?
   Bilbo is speaking to Thorin, who is laying wretchedly on the ground after being let out of his barrel.

3. The men of the town are skeptical of the old legends and put on a pretense of guarding the bridge from the dragon. Is their behavior an allegory of our society's lack of faith?
   Tolkien disliked allegory, so he probably did not mean for Lake-town to stand for our society. On the other hand, he did portray this suspicion of the men in a way that is applicable to our society's lack of faith.

Chapter 11

1. What is happening when the second quotation is said?
   Balin, Fili, Kili, and Bilbo are scouting out the land to the south of the Mountain, where the Front Gate stands.

2. Explain the meaning of this sentence: "They were at the end of their journey, but as far as ever, it seemed, from the end of their quest."
   Although they have reached their destination, they have a seemingly impossible task of getting inside and stealing back their wealth from Smaug.

3. What is the importance of this chapter title? Do you remember Bilbo's statement to the dwarves in Chapter 1? In this chapter, what is Bilbo's most important role?
   Bilbo had said, "If you sit on the doorstep long enough, I daresay you will think of something." They are now on that doorstep, and so that's the name of the chapter. Bilbo's most important role is figuring out how the secret gate opens.

Chapter 12

1. To whom is the first quotation directed?
   Bilbo

2. What is the weak point in the dwarves' plans? How does this tie in with the difference between a journey and a quest?
   They have never determined how to deal with Smaug. Unlike a journey, a quest has an end goal in mind, and they must think ahead how to achieve that goal.

3. The dwarves are anxious to reclaim their treasure. What begins to happen to the dwarves as they near the dragon's hoard?
   They come under the enchantment of the treasure hoard.

Chapter 13

1. What is the speaker talking about in the second quotation?
   Thorin is talking about Bilbo's cries for help after he had fallen and his light had gone out.

2. Do you have an idea where Smaug is? (Refer to the last paragraph of Chapter 12.) Why is Smaug away? Does the uncertainty of Smaug's whereabouts help to prepare us for what happens next?
   Smaug is likely preparing for his revenge; he'd headed in the direction of River Running. It causes suspense and raises the question "What will Smaug do?" Answers will vary.

Chapter 14

1. How had the information come to light in the third quotation?
   The thrush had heard Bilbo's news and information about Smaug, including his weak spot.

2. A company of archers does not give up the fight to defend their town. Bard has spent his last arrow but one, and he is alone. What happens next?
   The thrush comes with counsel about how to kill the dragon.

3. In the previous chapter, the dwarves sat outside the Mountain gate wondering about Smaug's absence and noticing the gathering of birds. How is this scene connected with the battle scene in Lake-town? Where are the birds mentioned next? Why did the author write two chapters about the same period of time?
   The scene outside the Mountain gate is two days after Smaug's defeat, and the birds are gathering about the recent events, probably led by the old thrush. The chapters involve the same period of time because the first one built suspense about the latter.

Chapter 15

1. What is the cause spoken about in the second quotation?
   The men of Lake-town had aided the dwarves in their distress, and so far the dwarves have not repaid them.

2. Read the dwarves' song. Go back to the first song. Combine the two. Do they tell a complete story? Which verse(s) of the second song are almost identical to the first? Now that the foe in the first song is dead, what foe is referred to in the new song?
   They tell the story of Smaug, but they start another one. The third and fourth verses are almost identical. The new foes are the armies of Esgaroth and the Elvenking gathered outside the dwarves' gates.

3. Do you think Bard's request for one-twelfth portion of the treasure is reasonable? Why does Thorin reject his claim? What do you think of Thorin and the dwarves? Is their behavior typical of human nature? Do you think their selfish cause will succeed? Explain.
   The amount Bard requests is fair since it includes his payment as dragon-slayer and heir of Girion, plus money he will give for the aid of Esgaroth. Thorin rejects the claim out of greed and pride. They have come under the gold's enchantment, which has increased in power over the years of the dragon's hoarding. The dwarves will not succeed because they are acting foolishly.

4. Why do you think the author ends this chapter with Bilbo's discontented thoughts? Try to guess what happens next. (See the title of the next chapter for a clue.)
   His thoughts indicate that he may do something to prevent the war that seems to be imminent.

Chapter 16

1. What effect upon Bilbo does the first quotation have?
   He is frightened, but he is also instigated to form a plan using the Arkenstone.

2. Why do you think Gandalf is pleased with Bilbo's plan? Is this another allusion to "predestination" or Providence? Bilbo chooses to do this of his own free will, yet Gandalf has been hoping this would be his choice. How does this interplay reveal Gandalf's position as prophet/angel?
   Gandalf is pleased because he had been the one to choose Bilbo for the task, and Bilbo is performing in an excellent way. This may be applicable to the idea of Providence, which teaches that people's actions are not accidental, but guided by the plan of God. Gandalf is like a prophet because he brings news, foretells something of the future, and provides encouragement.

Chapter 17

1. Who is the "descendant of rats" spoken to in the third quotation?
   Bilbo

2. In the last chapter, we discussed Bilbo's choice to give up his share of the treasure. Now we are seeing Thorin's side of things. Thorin accuses Bilbo of being a burglar, but that was his job description from the beginning. Discuss the irony of this accusation. What causes Thorin to turn against Bilbo? What causes Bilbo to do what he does?
   This is ironic because Bilbo has become a "reverse burglar," stealing from Thorin, as he sees it. Thorin sees Bilbo's actions as treachery, and his anger is fueled by his greed. Bilbo gives away the Arkenstone in order to prevent anyone from getting hurt and to make things right.

Chapter 18

1. What are the drawbacks of invisibility mentioned in the first quotation?
   Being invisible means Bilbo is missed by those searching for him after the battle.

Chapter 19

1. Throughout his journeys, Bilbo keeps the end in view: comfort and home. In your opinion, what would have happened to Bilbo had he arrived at Bag-End a few days too late?
   All his possessions would have been auctioned off and his home taken by the Sackville-Bagginses.

QUIZZES & TESTS
(Reproducible)

Poetry Exam: The Dwarves' Song

Name:______________________________ Date: ________________ Score: ______

Fill in the blank with the correct word from the poem. (1 point each)

1. Far over the misty mountains __________
2. To dungeons __________ and caverns old,
3. We must away ere break of __________,
4. To seek the pale ______________ gold.
5. The dwarves of __________ made mighty spells,
6. While ______________ fell like ringing bells
7. In places deep, where __________ things sleep,
8. In hollow halls beneath the __________.
9. For ancient king and ______________ lord
10. There many a gleaming golden ____________
11. They shaped and wrought, and ____________ they caught
12. To hide in gems on __________ of sword.
13. On silver necklaces they ____________
14. The flowering __________, on crowns they hung
15. The _____________-__________, in twisted wire
16. They meshed the light of moon and __________.
17. Far over the misty mountains __________
18. To dungeons __________ and caverns old,
19. We must away ere break of __________,
20. To claim our long-______________ gold.
21. _____________ they carved there for themselves
22. And harps of gold; where no man ____________
23. There lay they long, and many a __________
24. Was sung unheard by men or __________.
25. The pines were ____________ on the height,

26. The ____________ were moaning in the night.

27. The ____________ was red, it flaming spread;

28. The trees like ____________ blazed with light.

29. The bells were ringing in the ____________

30. And men looked up with ____________ pale;

31. Then dragon's ____________ more fierce than fire

32. Laid low their towers and houses ____________.

33. The mountain ____________ beneath the moon;

34. The dwarves, they heard the tramp of ____________.

35. They fled their ____________ to dying fall

36. Beneath his ____________, beneath the moon.

37. Far over the misty mountains ____________

38. To dungeons deep and caverns ____________,

39. We must away ere break of ____________,

40. To win our ____________ and gold from him!

Quiz 1: Chapters 1-4

Name:______________________________ Date: ______________ Score: ______

MATCHING: Match the character to its correct description. (1 point each)

________ 1. Bilbo Baggins	**A.**	a wizard who takes a hobbit on an adventure
________ 2. Gandalf	**B.**	a people of short, stout stature, with beards and a love of treasure
________ 3. dwarves	**C.**	an important dwarf leading a band of twelve other dwarves
________ 4. trolls	**D.**	cruel, wicked, bad-hearted creatures who live underground
________ 5. elves	**E.**	large creatures; not very clever, but dangerous and evil
________ 6. goblins	**F.**	a well-to-do hobbit from Hobbiton
________ 7. Thorin	**G.**	a wise and noble people who are merry and fair

MULTIPLE CHOICE: Use the map on the following page to answer the following questions. Circle the appropriate letter. (1 point each)

1. In the area labeled "A," which of the following occurs?
   a. A dragon destroys a small village.
   b. A wizard, dwarves, and a hobbit start an adventure.
   c. The Necromancer imprisons a dwarf.

2. In the area labeled "B," who discovered the secret of the Moon Letters?
   a. Glamdring
   b. Gandalf
   c. Elrond

3. In the area labeled "C," who caught the Company on their "front porch"?
   a. trolls
   b. goblins
   c. giants

4. In the area labeled "D," which of the following had happened to the dwarves?
   a. A dragon had stolen their home and treasure.
   b. They had made a living mining coal and doing blacksmith work.
   c. Trolls had tried to cook them.

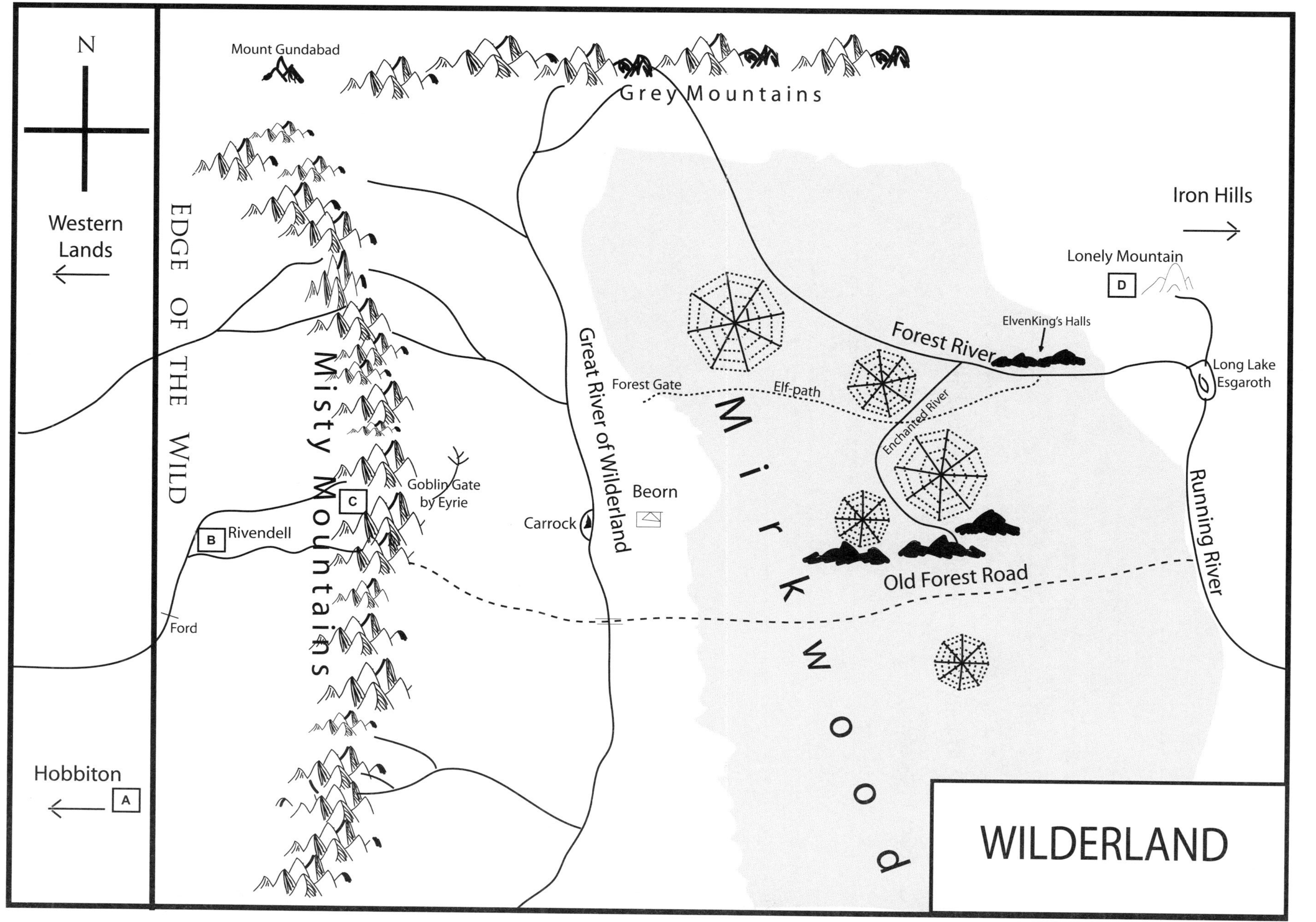
WILDERLAND
Iron Hills
Lonely Mountain
D
Long Lake
Esgaroth
Running River
ElvenKing's Halls
Forest River
Enchanted River
Old Forest Road
Mirkwood
Grey Mountains
Elf-path
Forest Gate
Beorn
Great River of Wilderland
Carrock
Goblin Gate
by Eyrie
C
Misty Mountains
Mount Gundabad
Rivendell
B
Edge of the Wild
Ford
N
Western Lands
Hobbiton
A

COMPREHENSION QUESTIONS: Answer the following in complete sentences. (14 points total)

1. The Tooks are richer than the Bagginses, but not as respectable. Why? Give an example. (4 pts.)

____

____

____

____

____

2. What causes Bilbo to leave his hobbit hole without his pocket-handkerchief, and where does he meet the Company of dwarves? (4 pts.)

____

____

____

____

____

3. While at Rivendell, Elrond discovers moon-letters on Thorin's map. What message do the moon-letters reveal? Write the message. (3 pts.)

____

____

____

____

____

4. The goblins fear two specific items that the Company possesses. What are these items? (3 pts.)

____

____

____

Quiz 2: Chapters 5-9

Name:______________________________ Date: ______________ Score: ________

MATCHING: Match the character to its correct description. (1 point each)

_________	**1.** Gollum	**A.** evil wolves that live over the Edge of the Wild
_________	**2.** wargs	**B.** proud, strong, noble-hearted birds that live in the Misty Mountains
_________	**3.** eagles	**C.** ruler in Mirkwood; good but stern
_________	**4.** Beorn	**D.** a terrible forest
_________	**5.** Mirkwood	**E.** a small, slimy, wicked creature living beneath the mountain
_________	**6.** Elvenking	**F.** the elves who lived in Mirkwood, in the home of the Elvenking
_________	**7.** Wood-elves	**G.** a good man living near Mirkwood who transforms into a bear

MULTIPLE CHOICE: Use the map on the following page to answer the following questions. Circle the appropriate letter. (1 point each)

1. In the area labeled "A," which of the following occurs?
   - **a.** The Company meets Beorn.
   - **b.** Wood-men attack the Company.
   - **c.** The Company escapes the goblins but encounter wargs, and are saved by eagles.

2. In the area labeled "B," who are the friends and servants of Beorn?
   - **a.** He lives alone.
   - **b.** animals
   - **c.** goblins he had taken prisoner

3. In the area labeled "C," which events occur?
   - **a.** The Company leaves Gandalf and quickly passes through Mirkwood.
   - **b.** Bombur falls in a river and the dwarves are captured by spiders.
   - **c.** Bilbo flies on the back of an eagle and meets the Elvenking.

4. In the area labeled "D," which of the following happens to the dwarves?
   - **a.** The Elvenking treats them to a merry feast.
   - **b.** Bilbo helps them escape through the Elvenking's front gate.
   - **c.** Bilbo sends them down the river in barrels.

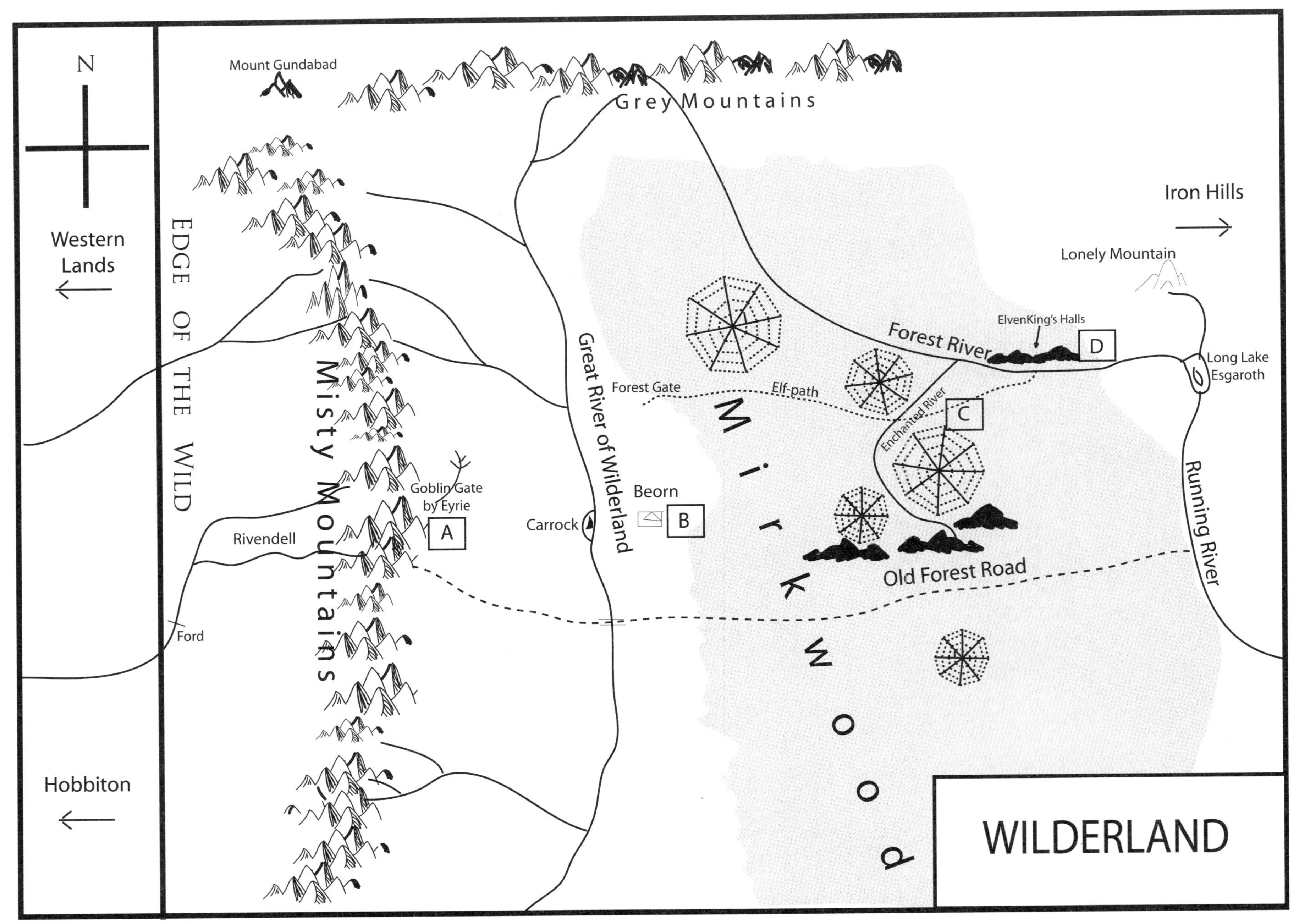
Mount Gundabad
Grey Mountains
N
Western
Lands
Iron Hills
Lonely Mountain
ElvenKing's Halls
Forest River
D
Long Lake
Esgaroth
EDGE OF THE WILD
Misty Mountains
Great River of Wilderland
Forest Gate
Elf-path
Enchanted River
C
Mirkwood
Goblin Gate
by Eyrie
A
Beorn
B
Carrock
Rivendell
Running River
Old Forest Road
Ford
Hobbiton
WILDERLAND

COMPREHENSION QUESTIONS: Answer the following in complete sentences. (14 points total)

1. Why does Gollum suggest a game of riddles? Which one of Bilbo's riddles is not really a riddle, and how does Gollum react? (3 pts.)

2. What improves Bilbo's reputation with the Company? (3 pts.)

3. In Mirkwood, what lures the dwarves off the Elf-path? Why and how does this happen? (4 pts.)

4. Briefly explain how Bilbo helps the Company escape from the Elvenking. (4 pts.)

Midterm Exam: Chapters 1-9

Name:____ Date: __________________ Score: _______

WHO SAID IT?: Give the name of the speaker(s) for each quotation. (1 point each)

_____________________ 1. *"I am looking for someone to share in an adventure that I am arranging, and it's very difficult to find anyone."*

_____________________ 2. *"We are plain quiet folk and I have no use for adventures. Nasty disturbing uncomfortable things! Make you late for dinner!"*

_____________________ 3. *"Tell me what you want done, and I will try it, if I have to walk from here to the East of East and fight the wild Were-worms in the Last Desert!"*

_____________________ 4. *"Blimey, Bert, look what I've copped!"*

_____________________ 5. *"I am a good cook myself, and cook better than I cook, if you see what I mean."*

_____________________ 6. *"Hmmm! It smells like elves!"*

_____________________ 7. *"Stand by the grey stone when the thrush knocks, and the setting sun with the last light of Durin's Day will shine upon the key-hole."*

_____________________ 8. *"Who are these miserable persons?"*

_____________________ 9. *"Why, O why did I ever bring a wretched little hobbit on a treasure hunt!"*

_____________________ 10. *"Is it nice, my preciousss? Is it juicy? Is it scrumptiously crunchable?"*

_____________________ 11. *"A very ticklish business, it was. Touch and go!"*

_____________________ 12. *"A dozen! That's the first time I've heard eight called a dozen."*

_____________________ 13. *"I will give you a name and I shall call you Sting."*

_____________________ 14. *"There is no escape from my magic doors for those who are once brought inside."*

_____________________ 15. *"We shall be bruised and battered to pieces, and drowned too, for certain!"*

MULTIPLE CHOICE: Choose the correct response and circle the answer. (1 point each)

1. The Took side of Bilbo's family was not as respectable as the Bagginses because:
   - **a.** They were part fairy.
   - **b.** They were poorer.
   - **c.** They were adventurous.

2. The dwarves were planning to:
   - **a.** visit their relatives in Moria
   - **b.** seek their treasure
   - **c.** fight goblins

3. Bill, Bert, and Tom kept these items in their lair:
   - **a.** supplies and treasures
   - **b.** sheep
   - **c.** prisoners

4. Elrond told the Company valuable information about:
   - **a.** how to fight dragons
   - **b.** the map and the swords
   - **c.** the spiders in Mirkwood

5. Thorin told the Great Goblin that they were traveling to:
   a. return home after a long absence
   b. win back treasure
   c. visit relatives

6. Gollum suggested a game of riddles in order to:
   a. learn about Bilbo
   b. to keep Bilbo's company
   c. to pass the time

7. Immediately after fleeing the mountain, the Company stumbled into:
   a. a party of elves
   b. a gathering of wolves
   c. an eagle's eyrie

8. Beorn came to like the dwarves because they:
   a. killed goblins
   b. came with Gandalf
   c. sang interesting songs

9. The dwarves were lured off the path in Mirkwood by:
   a. fear of spiders
   b. elvish magic
   c. hunger and desperation

10. The chief value in Bilbo's invisibility in the Elvenking's palace was that he was able to:
   a. steal food
   b. encourage the dwarves
   c. devise a plan of escape

VOCABULARY USAGE: Fill in the blank with the appropriate vocabulary word. (1 point each)

bulbous	eyrie	flummoxed	glowered	paraphernalia	precipice	purloined

1. The librarian ________________ at the rowdy students as they noisily disrupted the quiet environment of the library. (v.)

2. The large bird's ________________ had been cleverly fashioned with twigs, grass, and mud. (n.)

3. The thief had to return each item he had ________________ when he was caught red-handed by the store owner. (v.)

4. The man's ________________ nose was swollen and red as he sneezed into his handkerchief. (adj.)

5. Every year the baseball team hires a team manager to corral the various ________________ needed for each game. (n.)

6. The man was ________________ when the doorbell rang, as he was not expecting any visitors. (adj.)

7. The base jumper stood precariously on the ________________ as he eagerly awaited the signal to jump from his instructor. (n.)

ESSAY: Give good, complete answers, using full sentences and perfect punctuation. (5 points each)

1. Describe the two sides of Bilbo's personality or disposition as they relate to his mother's and father's sides of the family.

2. Compare and contrast these three races: hobbits, dwarves, and elves.

3. Tell how Bilbo has begun to prove these words of Gandalf: "I have chosen Mr. Baggins and that ought to be enough for all of you. … There is a lot more in him than you guess, and a deal more than he has any idea of himself."

Quiz 3: Chapters 10-14

Name:____ Date: __________________ Score: _______

MATCHING: Match the character to its correct description. (1 point each)

_________ **1.** Lake-town		**A.** ruler of Lake-town; a shrewd and wary man
_________ **2.** Dale		**B.** the large black bird that lives near the mountain
_________ **3.** Master		**C.** cavernous opening at Mountain's foot; source of Running River
_________ **4.** Ravenhill		**D.** a once-thriving town near the Mountain
_________ **5.** Front Gate		**E.** a town on the surface of the Long Lake
_________ **6.** Bard		**F.** a grim man descended from Lord Girion of Dale
_________ **7.** thrush		**G.** a watch tower on the southern spur of the Mountain

MULTIPLE CHOICE: Use the map on the following page to answer the following questions. Circle the appropriate letter. (1 point each)

1. In the area labeled "A," which of the following occurs?

- **a.** The Company rides in boats from the Elvenking's halls.
- **b.** The dwarves and Bilbo are welcomed and aided by the men of Lake-town.
- **c.** Gandalf joins the Company again.

2. In the area labeled "B," what does Bilbo do?

- **a.** He leads the dwarves through the Front Gate.
- **b.** He has a conversation with Smaug.
- **c.** He shoots an arrow into the dragon's weak spot.

3. In the area labeled "A," who do we meet for the first time?

- **a.** Bard
- **b.** the Elvenking
- **c.** Smaug the dragon

4. In the area labeled "B," which of the following is guarded?

- **a.** the ring of invisibility
- **b.** the crown of Durin
- **c.** the Arkenstone

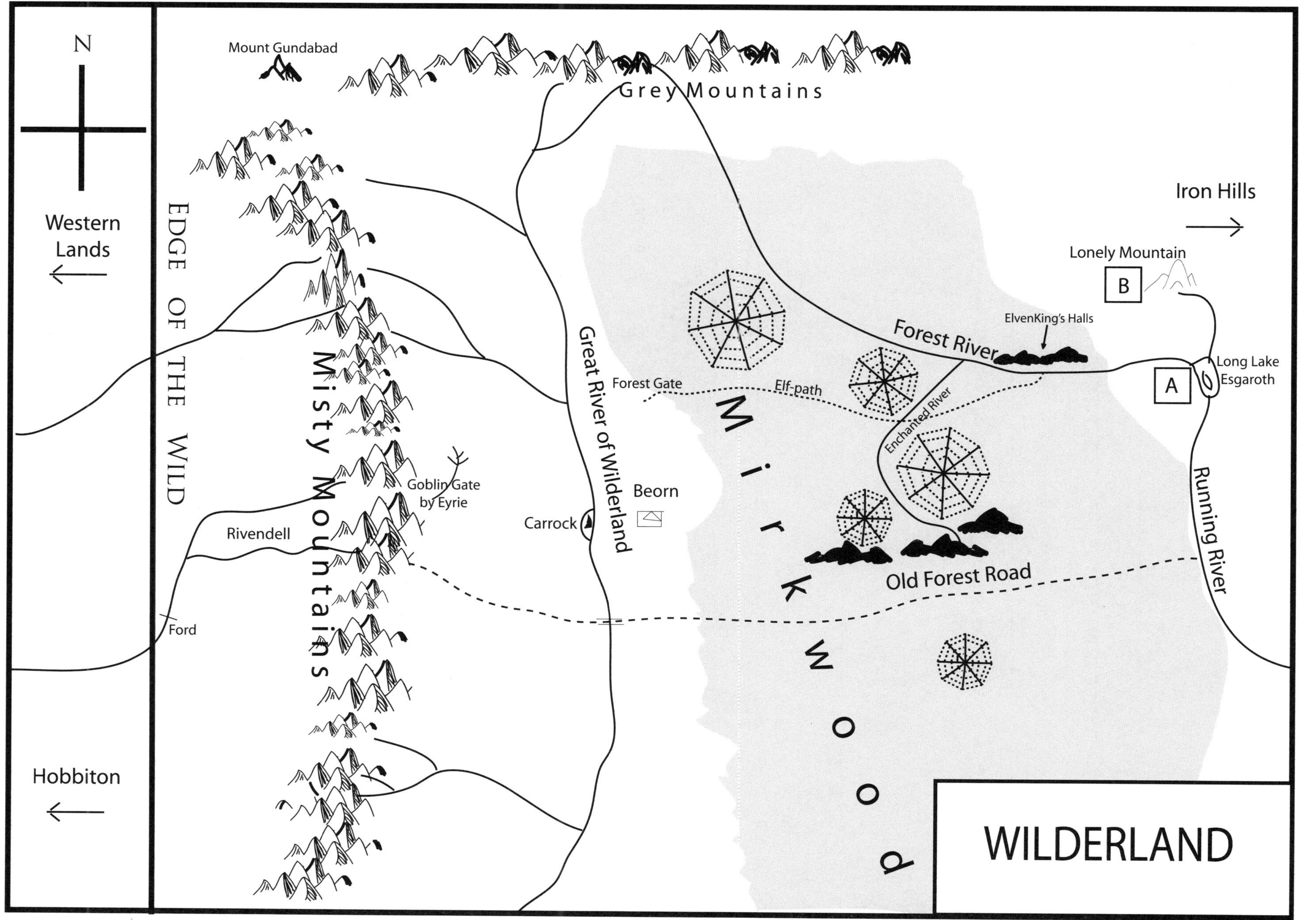

N
Western
Lands
Hobbiton
Mount Gundabad
Grey Mountains
EDGE OF THE WILD
Misty Mountains
Goblin Gate
by Eyrie
Rivendell
Ford
Great River of Wilderland
Carrock
Beorn
Forest Gate
Elf-path
Mirkwood
Enchanted River
Forest River
ElvenKing's Halls
Old Forest Road
Iron Hills
Lonely Mountain
B
A
Long Lake
Esgaroth
Running River
WILDERLAND

COMPREHENSION QUESTIONS: Answer the following in complete sentences. (14 points total)

1. What methods do the dwarves use to attempt to open the door? Why do you think they are not successful? (3 pts.)

2. How does Bilbo trick Smaug into revealing his weak spot, and what is it? (4 pts.)

3. What does Bilbo find while searching through the treasure, what does he do with it, and what does he say about himself? (4 pts.)

4. What does the mere glimpse of the treasure rekindle in the hearts of the dwarves? Does this urge them on through the cavern? (3 pts.)

Quiz 4: Chapters 15-19

Name:____ Date: __________________ Score: _______

MATCHING: Match the character to its correct description. (1 point each)

_________ 1. Roac

_________ 2. Dain

_________ 3. Dwarf and Goblin Wars

_________ 4. Bolg of the North

_________ 5. The Battle of Five Armies

A. a battle of goblins and wargs against men, elves, and dwarves

B. Thorin's cousin and chief of the dwarves of the Iron Hills

C. chief of the great ravens of the Mountain; son of Carc

D. goblin ruler whose father Dain had killed in the Goblin Wars

E. seven-year war in which dwarves hunted goblins

MULTIPLE CHOICE: Use the map on the following page to answer the following questions. Circle the appropriate letter. (1 point each)

1. Who comes from the area labeled "E"?
   - **a.** Dain and his army
   - **b.** Bolg and his army
   - **c.** the eagles

2. Who comes from the area labeled "C"?
   - **a.** Dain and his army
   - **b.** Bolg and his army
   - **c.** the eagles

3. In the area labeled "D," what occurs?
   - **a.** Bilbo kills many goblins and wargs.
   - **b.** Bilbo is knocked unconscious and the enemy doesn't notice him.
   - **c.** Bilbo loses the Arkenstone.

4. In the area labeled "B," what does Bilbo learn regarding Gandalf's absence?
   - **a.** that Gandalf had been gone fighting the Necromancer in Mirkwood.
   - **b.** that Gandalf was helping summon Dain for reinforcements.
   - **c.** that Gandalf was fighting large wicked spiders in Mirkwood.

5. In the area labeled "A," what has happened?
   - **a.** Trolls have invaded.
   - **b.** Bilbo has been presumed dead.
   - **c.** A search has begun for Bilbo.

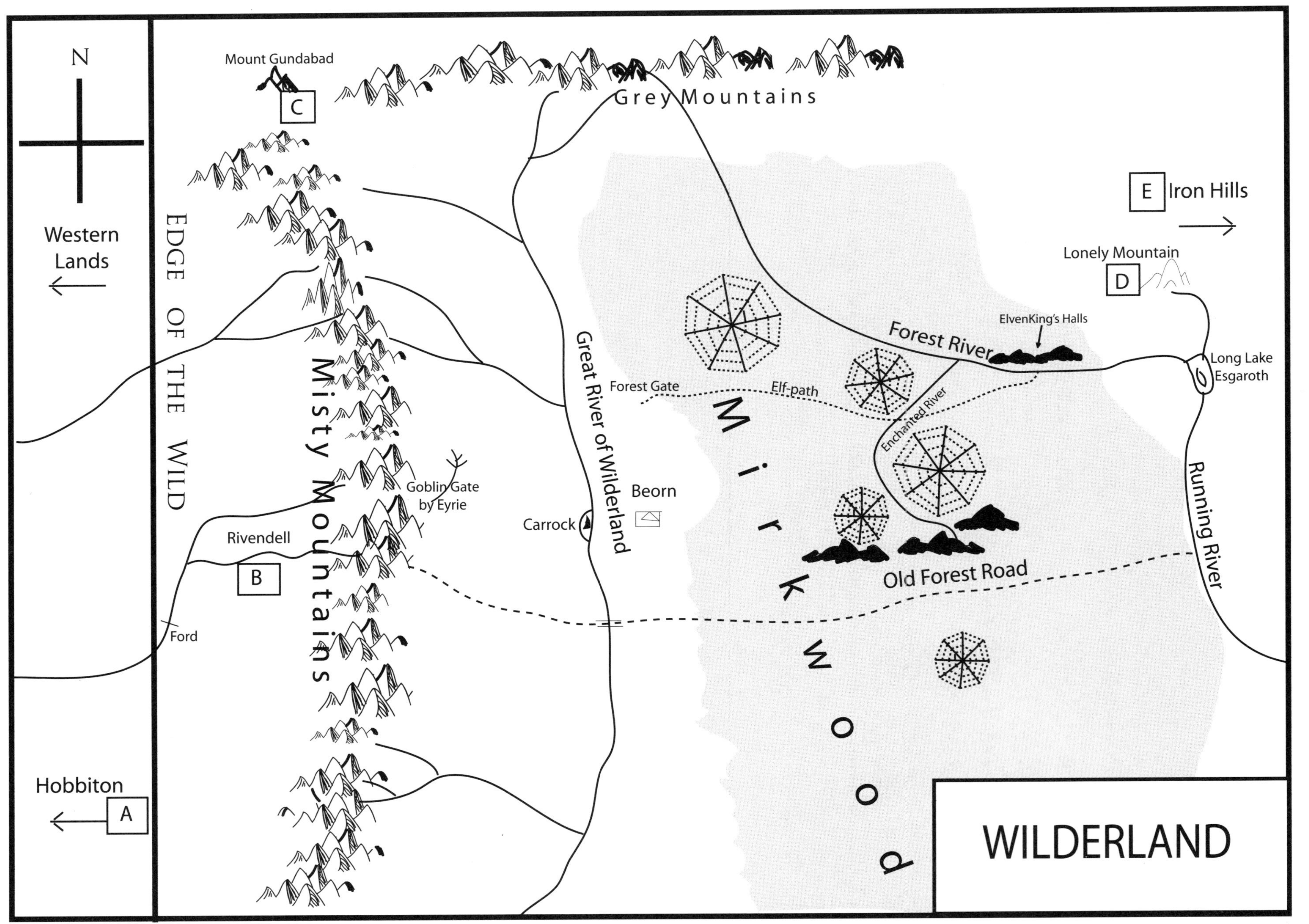
WILDERLAND
Mount Gundabad
C
Grey Mountains
E
Iron Hills
Western
Lands
EDGE OF THE WILD
Misty Mountains
Lonely Mountain
D
ElvenKing's Halls
Forest River
Long Lake
Esgaroth
Forest Gate
Elf-path
Enchanted River
Great River of Wilderland
Mirkwood
Goblin Gate
by Eyrie
Beorn
Carrock
Running River
Rivendell
B
Old Forest Road
Ford
Hobbiton
A
N

COMPREHENSION QUESTIONS: Answer the following in complete sentences. (15 points total)

1. Describe Roac. What is the message he delivers to Thorin? (3 pts.)

2. Thorin is obsessed with finding the Arkenstone. Where does Bilbo have it concealed, and how is it used when he negotiates with the enemy armies? (4 pts.)

3. Who is waiting to say farewell to Bilbo? How does their meeting end? (4 pts.)

4. Where does Bilbo finally get a pocket-handkerchief? What meaning do you think the author intended for this little detail in the story? (4 pts.)

Final Exam: Chapters 10-19

Name:________________________________ Date: ________________ Score: ______

WHO SAID IT?: Give the name of the speaker(s) for each quotation. (1 point each)

______________ 1. *"Well, are you alive or are you dead?"*

______________ 2. *"Who are you and what do you want?"*

______________ 3. *"Very well! We'll see! No treasure will come back through Mirkwood without my having something to say in the matter."*

______________ 4. *"There lies all that is left of Dale."*

______________ 5. *"I am too fat for such fly-walks. I should turn dizzy and tread on my beard, and then you would be thirteen again."*

______________ 6. *"You said sitting on the doorstep and thinking would be my job ..."*

______________ 7. *"Well, thief! I smell you and I feel your air."*

______________ 8. *"Never laugh at live dragons!"*

______________ 9. *"The Arkenstone! The Arkenstone!"*

______________ 10. *"They shall see me and remember who is the real King under the Mountain!"*

______________ 11. *"Now what on earth or under it has happened?"*

______________ 12. *"Don't call my palace a nasty hole! You wait till it has been cleaned and redecorated!"*

______________ 13. *"The dragon is coming or I am a fool!"*

______________ 14. *"Up the Bowman, and down with Moneybags!"*

______________ 15. *"You put your worst cause last and in the chief place."*

______________ 16. *"I would give a good deal for the feel of grass at my toes."*

______________ 17. *"Well done! Mr. Baggins! There is always more about you than anyone expects!"*

______________ 18. *"If you don't like my Burglar, please don't damage him."*

______________ 19. *"You all seem in league! What have you got to say, you descendant of rats?"*

______________ 20. *"Long will I tarry, ere I begin this war for gold."*

______________ 21. *"The eagles are coming!"*

______________ 22. *"There is more in you of good than you know, child of the kindly West."*

______________ 23. *"There let it lie till the Mountain falls!"*

______________ 24. *"And your snores would waken a stone dragon."*

______________ 25. *"My dear Bilbo! Something is the matter with you! You are not the hobbit that you were."*

MULTIPLE CHOICE: Choose the correct response and circle the answer. (1 point each)

1. The first dwarf out of his barrel was recognized by his:
   - **a.** blue hood, silver belt
   - **b.** white beard, scarlet hood
   - **c.** sky-blue hood, gold chain

2. Most people in Lake-town thought the dwarves were:
   - **a.** vagabonds and tramps
   - **b.** fulfilling a prophecy
   - **c.** lying about their story

3. When they could not open the secret door, the dwarves:
   - **a.** blamed Bilbo
   - **b.** went in the Front Gate
   - **c.** decided to give up

4. Bilbo remembered the message of the runes because:
   - **a.** a thrush appeared
   - **b.** the moon shone
   - **c.** a pebble fell on his head

5. When Bilbo went down the tunnel toward Smaug, it was:
   - **a.** damp and clammy
   - **b.** his bravest act
   - **c.** blocked by fallen stone

6. Bilbo stole this on his first visit to Smaug:
   - **a.** the Arkenstone
   - **b.** silver armor
   - **c.** a cup

7. Looking at Smaug's waistcoat of diamonds, Bilbo saw:
   - **a.** the Arkenstone
   - **b.** a weak spot
   - **c.** an impenetrable defense

8. When Bilbo found the Arkenstone, he:
   - **a.** gave it to Thorin
   - **b.** put it in his pocket
   - **c.** hid it under a rock

9. The dwarves and Bilbo were in the Mountain for:
   - **a.** a whole day and a night
   - **b.** five days
   - **c.** two nights and a day

10. Because his treasure had been thieved, Smaug blamed:
    - **a.** the men of Lake-town
    - **b.** the elves of Mirkwood
    - **c.** the dwarves of Esgaroth

11. The Elvenking gathered his army to march for:
    - **a.** an attack on Smaug
    - **b.** the rebuilding of Lake-town
    - **c.** the Mountain

12. This person told Thorin about the death of Smaug and the gathering of armies:
    - **a.** Roac
    - **b.** Carc
    - **c.** Cram

13. Thorin sent messengers to Dain hoping for help to:
    - **a.** carry away the treasure
    - **b.** fight off goblins
    - **c.** guard the gold for themselves

14. Bilbo's displeasure with the situation between Thorin and Bard forced him to:
    - **a.** call Gandalf to his aid
    - **b.** give away the Arkenstone
    - **c.** go back home

15. The Elvenking did not want:

a. to fight over gold

b. to let the dwarves win

c. Bilbo to fight in battle

16. The turning point of the battle was:

a. the onslaught of wargs

b. Thorin's entry

c. the eagles' arrival

17. When Bilbo was found, Gandalf took him to:

a. see Thorin

b. get food and drink

c. rest in the camp

18. A chest of silver and a chest of gold were given to:

a. Dain

b. Bilbo

c. the Elvenking

19. Gandalf had left the Company at the gate to Mirkwood in order to:

a. warn the wood-men

b. fight the Necromancer

c. learn from the White Council

20. Upon arriving back in Hobbiton, Bilbo found that he had lost:

a. his best set of forks

b. his magic ring

c. most of the hobbits' respect

FILL IN THE BLANK: Fill in the blank with the correct word. (1 point each)

1. The dwarves came out of the barrels once they arrived at ________________.

2. The ________________ of Lake-town helped the dwarves, but hoped they'd leave.

3. When the Company left Lake-town, the only gloomy person was ________________.

4. From the Front Gate of the Lonely Mountain runs the ________________ River.

5. The town in ruins that stands near the Mountain was called ________________.

6. The secret door was found by Fili, Kili, and ________________.

7. Bilbo called himself Ringwinner, Luckwearer, and ________________-rider.

8. Smaug could not see Bilbo because of the magic ________________.

9. The Arkenstone was known as the ________________ of the Mountain.

10. Thorin dressed ________________ in a coat of silver-steel called mithril.

11. The warning of Smaug's attack on Lake-town was sounded by ________________.

12. The Master blamed the ________________ for Smaug's attack.

13. The ________________ and his army stopped to help the men of Lake-town rebuild.

14. Thorin's cousin living in the Iron Hills was ________________.

15. Bard argued with _______________ to give some of the treasure to men and elves.

16. Thorin was kept from throwing Bilbo off the wall by _______________.

17. _______________ of the North attacked the Mountain with goblins and wargs.

18. _______________ killed the goblin chief and ensured the victory.

19. On the return journey, Gandalf and Bilbo visited Elrond's home, _________________________.

20. The old ____________________ had caught the dragon-sickness and come to a bad end.

VOCABULARY USAGE: Fill in the blank with the appropriate vocabulary word. (1 point each)

antiquated	lore	implored	glowered	eyrie	flummoxed	promontory
purloined	precipice	pallid	succoured	bulbous	deposed	paraphernalia

1. The medic _______________ the wounded, even in the most dangerous of circumstances. (v.)

2. The fans _______________ as they watched their favorite sports team lose the game to their rival. (v.)

3. The clothing exhibit in the museum modeled _______________ styles from the 1800s. (adj.)

4. The young boy's face turned _______________ as the menacing dog came closer. (adj.)

5. Darting its _______________ eyes back and forth, the chameleon quickly changed color to avoid being seen by the predator. (adj.)

6. The ruler was _______________ as a result of his unjust and immoral practices. (v.)

7. The aged lighthouse stood at the end of a long _______________ overlooking the sea. (n.)

8. While hiking, a group of adventurous teenagers stumbled upon an abandoned _______________ that clearly had been home to a large bird. (n.)

9. Any retelling of Greek mythological _______________ must include the story of Perseus killing the Gorgon, Medusa. (n.)

10. Before going to bed, the girl collected the necessary ____________________ for the next day's activities. (n.)

11. The student, _______________ by the verb endings, could not accurately conjugate the verb. (adj.)

12. Though strictly commanded by the general not to, the soldier _______________ gold, silver, and a beautiful garment during the attack on the enemy's city. (v.)

13. With tears in her eyes, the little girl _______________ her dad to reconsider letting her have a puppy for her birthday. (v.)

14. Standing on the _______________ of the Grand Canyon, the tourist was able to see a vast panorama of beauty. (n.)

ESSAY: Give good, complete answers, using full sentences and perfect punctuation. (5 points each)

1. Compare and contrast Bard and the Master; how are they alike, how are they different?

2. Describe the effect that the dragon's enchanted hoard had on Bilbo, Thorin, and the old Master of Lake-town.

3. At the end of the story, Gandalf says, "You are a very fine person, Mr. Baggins, and I am very fond of you; but you are only quite a little fellow in a wide world after all!" Bilbo responds by saying, "Thank goodness!" and laughs happily. Why is Gandalf's comment not a put-down but an encouragement?

QUIZZES & TESTS KEY

Poetry Exam: The Dwarves' Song — KEY

Name:______________________________ Date: ________________ Score: ______

Fill in the blank with the correct word from the poem. (1 point each)

1. Far over the misty mountains cold
2. To dungeons deep and caverns old,
3. We must away ere break of day,
4. To seek the pale enchanted gold.
5. The dwarves of yore made mighty spells,
6. While hammers fell like ringing bells
7. In places deep, where dark things sleep,
8. In hollow halls beneath the fells.
9. For ancient king and elvish lord
10. There many a gleaming golden hoard
11. They shaped and wrought, and light they caught
12. To hide in gems on hilt of sword.
13. On silver necklaces they strung
14. The flowering stars, on crowns they hung
15. The dragon-fire, in twisted wire
16. They meshed the light of moon and sun.
17. Far over the misty mountains cold
18. To dungeons deep and caverns old,
19. We must away ere break of day,
20. To claim our long-forgotten gold.
21. Goblets they carved there for themselves
22. And harps of gold; where no man delves
23. There lay they long, and many a song
24. Was sung unheard by men or elves.
25. The pines were roaring on the height,

26. The ___winds___ were moaning in the night.

27. The ___fire___ was red, it flaming spread;

28. The trees like ___torches___ blazed with light.

29. The bells were ringing in the ___dale___

30. And men looked up with ___faces___ pale;

31. Then dragon's ___ire___ more fierce than fire

32. Laid low their towers and houses ___frail___.

33. The mountain ___smoked___ beneath the moon;

34. The dwarves, they heard the tramp of ___doom___.

35. They fled their ___hall___ to dying fall

36. Beneath his ___feet___, beneath the moon.

37. Far over the misty mountains ___grim___

38. To dungeons deep and caverns ___dim___,

39. We must away ere break of ___day___,

40. To win our ___harps___ and gold from him!

Quiz 1: Chapters 1-4 — KEY

Name:________________________ Date: ______________ Score: ______

MATCHING: Match the character to its correct description. (1 point each)

F 1. Bilbo Baggins
A 2. Gandalf
B 3. dwarves
E 4. trolls
G 5. elves
D 6. goblins
C 7. Thorin

A. a wizard who takes a hobbit on an adventure
B. a people of short, stout stature, with beards and a love of treasure
C. an important dwarf leading a band of twelve other dwarves
D. cruel, wicked, bad-hearted creatures who live underground
E. large creatures; not very clever, but dangerous and evil
F. a well-to-do hobbit from Hobbiton
G. a wise and noble people who are merry and fair

MULTIPLE CHOICE: Use the map on the following page to answer the following questions. Circle the appropriate letter. (1 point each)

1. In the area labeled "A," which of the following occurs?
   - a. A dragon destroys a small village.
   - **(b.)** A wizard, dwarves, and a hobbit start an adventure.
   - c. The Necromancer imprisons a dwarf.

2. In the area labeled "B," who discovered the secret of the Moon Letters?
   - a. Glamdring
   - b. Gandalf
   - **(c.)** Elrond

3. In the area labeled "C," who caught the Company on their "front porch"?
   - a. trolls
   - **(b.)** goblins
   - c. giants

4. In the area labeled "D," which of the following had happened to the dwarves?
   - **(a.)** A dragon had stolen their home and treasure.
   - b. They had made a living mining coal and doing blacksmith work.
   - c. Trolls had tried to cook them.

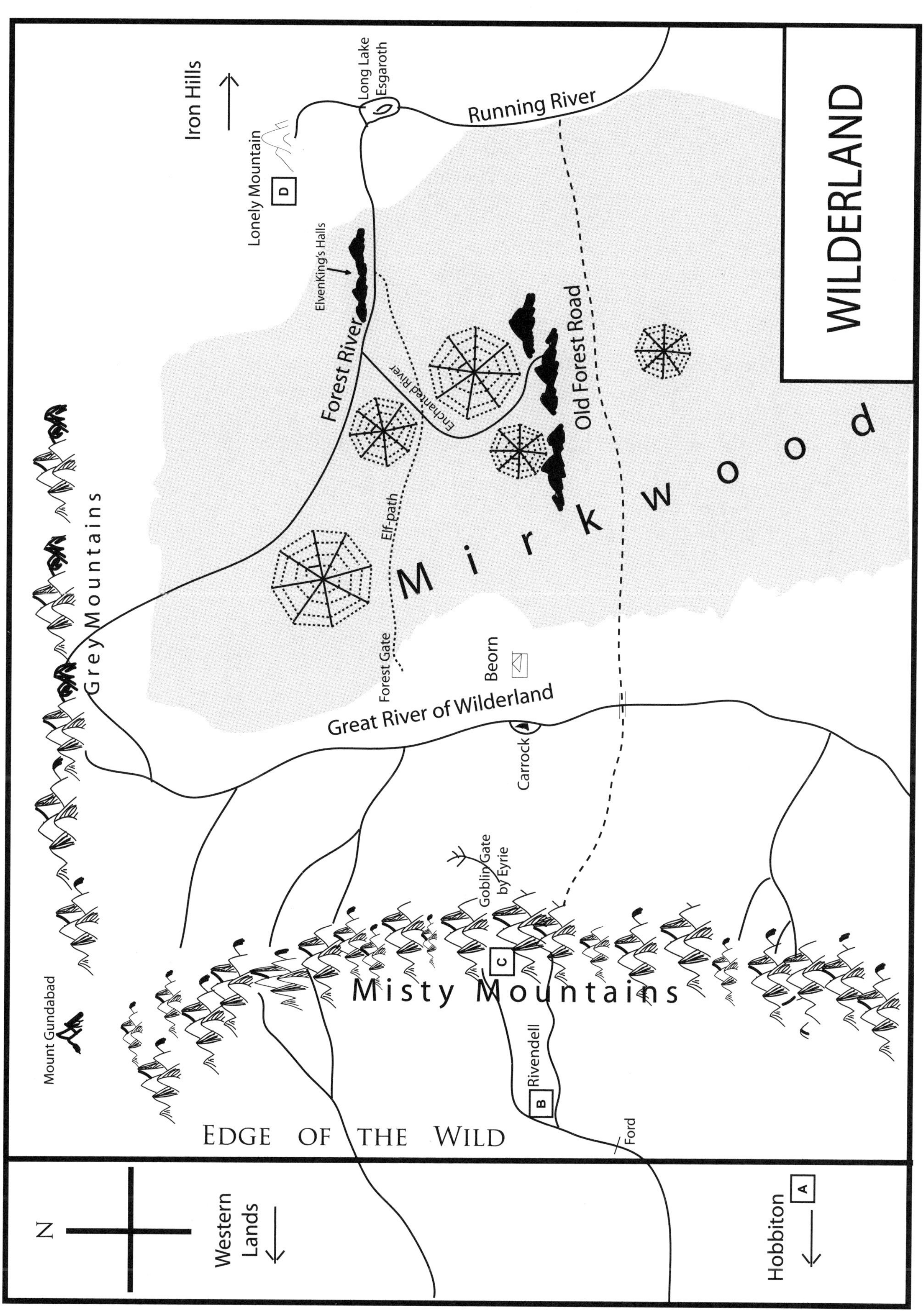

WILDERLAND
Iron Hills
Lonely Mountain
D
Long Lake
Esgaroth
Running River
ElvenKing's Halls
Forest River
Enchanted River
Old Forest Road
Mirkwood
Elf-path
Forest Gate
Beorn
Grey Mountains
Great River of Wilderland
Carrock
Goblin Gate by Eyrie
C
Misty Mountains
Mount Gundabad
Rivendell
B
EDGE OF THE WILD
Ford
N
Western Lands
Hobbiton
A

COMPREHENSION QUESTIONS: Answer the following in complete sentences. (14 points total)

1. The Tooks are richer than the Bagginses, but not as respectable. Why? Give an example. (4 pts.)

   One of the Took ancestors is said to have taken a fairy wife. They are also known for going on adventures, which is not like hobbits to do. Hobbits are sensible and enjoy the comfort of their homes.

2. What causes Bilbo to leave his hobbit hole without his pocket-handkerchief, and where does he meet the Company of dwarves? (4 pts.)

   Thorin's letter that was left on the mantelpiece just under the clock and Gandalf pushing Bilbo out the door cause Bilbo to leave without his pocket-handkerchief. Bilbo meets the Company at the Inn of the Green Dragon.

3. While at Rivendell, Elrond discovers moon-letters on Thorin's map. What message do the moon-letters reveal? Write the message. (3 pts.)

   The moon's light reveals a magic rune message: "Stand by the grey stone when thrush knocks, and the setting sun with the last light of Durin's Day will shine upon the key-hole."

4. The goblins fear two specific items that the Company possesses. What are these items? (3 pts.)

   The goblins are afraid of the swords Glamdring (the Foe-hammer) and Orcrist (the Goblin-cleaver), which they call Beater and Biter.

Quiz 2: Chapters 5-9 — KEY

Name:______________________________ Date: ______________ Score: ________

MATCHING: Match the character to its correct description. (1 point each)

E	**1.** Gollum	**A.** evil wolves that live over the Edge of the Wild
A	**2.** wargs	**B.** proud, strong, noble-hearted birds that live in the Misty Mountains
B	**3.** eagles	**C.** ruler in Mirkwood; good but stern
G	**4.** Beorn	**D.** a terrible forest
D	**5.** Mirkwood	**E.** a small, slimy, wicked creature living beneath the mountain
C	**6.** Elvenking	**F.** the elves who lived in Mirkwood, in the home of the Elvenking
F	**7.** Wood-elves	**G.** a good man living near Mirkwood who transforms into a bear

MULTIPLE CHOICE: Use the map on the following page to answer the following questions. Circle the appropriate letter. (1 point each)

1. In the area labeled "A," which of the following occurs?

- **a.** The Company meets Beorn.
- **b.** Wood-men attack the Company.
- **(c.)** The Company escapes the goblins but encounter wargs, and are saved by eagles.

2. In the area labeled "B," who are the friends and servants of Beorn?

- **a.** He lives alone.
- **(b.)** animals
- **c.** goblins he had taken prisoner

3. In the area labeled "C," which events occur?

- **a.** The Company leaves Gandalf and quickly passes through Mirkwood.
- **(b.)** Bombur falls in a river and the dwarves are captured by spiders.
- **c.** Bilbo flies on the back of an eagle and meets the Elvenking.

4. In the area labeled "D," which of the following happens to the dwarves?

- **a.** The Elvenking treats them to a merry feast.
- **b.** Bilbo helps them escape through the Elvenking's front gate.
- **(c.)** Bilbo sends them down the river in barrels.

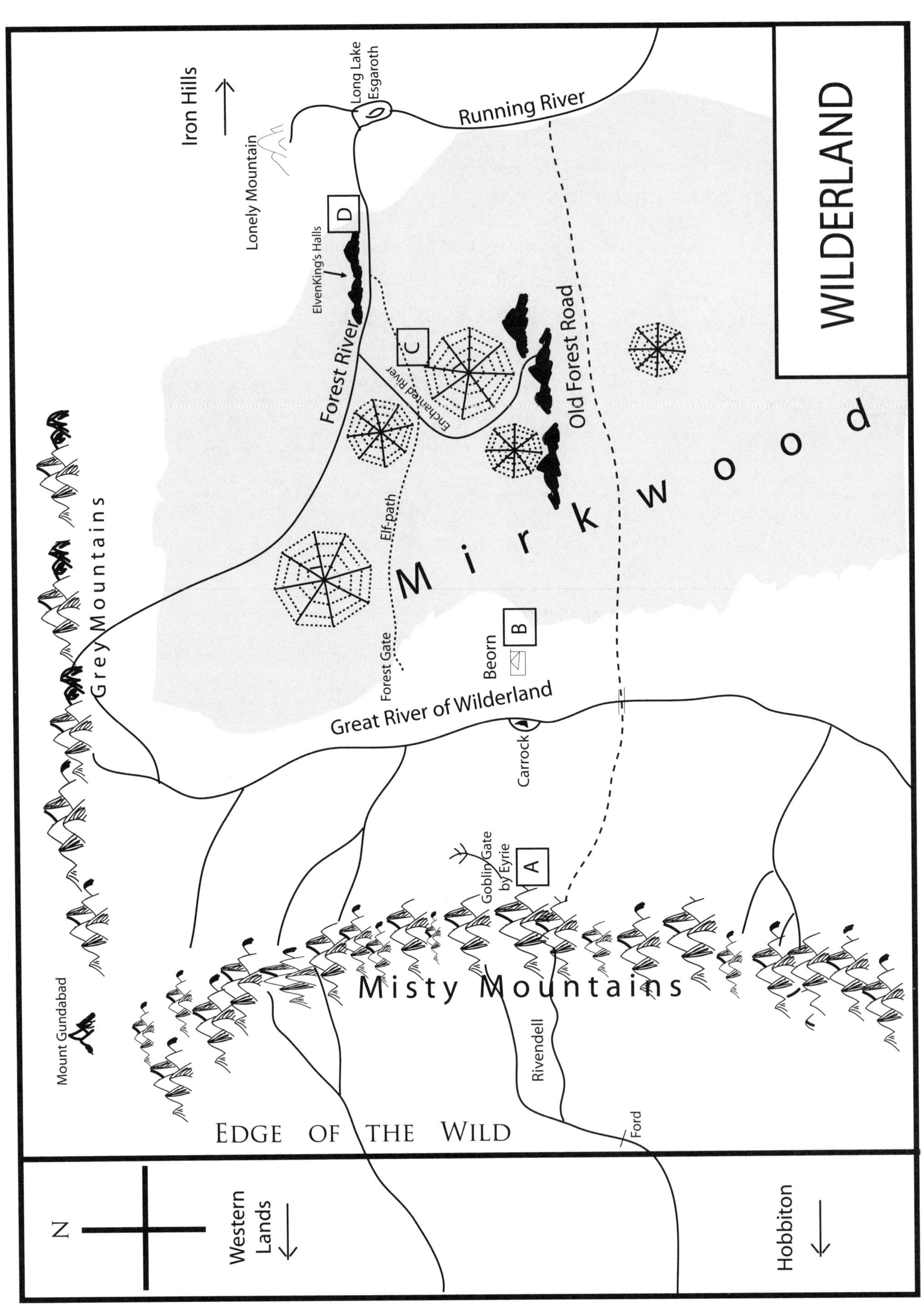
WILDERLAND
Iron Hills
Long Lake
Esgaroth
Running River
Lonely Mountain
D
ElvenKing's Halls
Forest River
C
Enchanted River
Old Forest Road
Mirkwood
Elf-path
Grey Mountains
Forest Gate
Beorn
B
Great River of Wilderland
Carrock
Goblin Gate
by Eyrie
A
Misty Mountains
Mount Gundabad
Rivendell
Ford
EDGE OF THE WILD
N
Western
Lands
Hobbiton

COMPREHENSION QUESTIONS: Answer the following in complete sentences. (14 points total)

1. Why does Gollum suggest a game of riddles? Which one of Bilbo's riddles is not really a riddle, and how does Gollum react? (3 pts.)

   It is the only game he knows, and he wants to find out more about Bilbo. Bilbo asks, "What have I got in my pocket?" This is not really a riddle. When Gollum cannot answer the question correctly, he gets very upset, hissing, spluttering, wriggling, and squirming.

2. What improves Bilbo's reputation with the Company? (3 pts.)

   The Company is impressed by Bilbo's surprise appearance and his escape from the goblins.

3. In Mirkwood, what lures the dwarves off the Elf-path? Why and how does this happen? (4 pts.)

   Hunger and desperation lure them off the path. They see fire from the Wood-elves' feast and hope to get food and help in finding their way out of Mirkwood. This is when they are attacked by spiders.

4. Briefly explain how Bilbo helps the Company escape from the Elvenking. (4 pts.)

   By wearing his ring, Bilbo stays invisible and discovers from the elves that the only way out of the palace is through the River Gate. He devises a plan to take the guard's keys after he falls asleep and then stuff the dwarves into barrels and float down the river through the River Gate, to freedom.

Midterm Exam: Chapters 1-9 — KEY

Name:________________________ Date: ______________ Score: ______

WHO SAID IT?: Give the name of the speaker(s) for each quotation. (1 point each)

Speaker	Quotation
Gandalf	1. *"I am looking for someone to share in an adventure that I am arranging, and it's very difficult to find anyone."*
Bilbo	2. *"We are plain quiet folk and I have no use for adventures. Nasty disturbing uncomfortable things! Make you late for dinner!"*
Bilbo	3. *"Tell me what you want done, and I will try it, if I have to walk from here to the East of East and fight the wild Were-worms in the Last Desert!"*
William	4. *"Blimey, Bert, look what I've copped!"*
Bilbo	5. *"I am a good cook myself, and cook better than I cook, if you see what I mean."*
Bilbo	6. *"Hmmm! It smells like elves!"*
Elrond	7. *"Stand by the grey stone when the thrush knocks, and the setting sun with the last light of Durin's Day will shine upon the key-hole."*
Great Goblin	8. *"Who are these miserable persons?"*
Bombur	9. *"Why, O why did I ever bring a wretched little hobbit on a treasure hunt!"*
Gollum	10. *"Is it nice, my preciousss? Is it juicy? Is it scrumptiously crunchable?"*
Gandalf	11. *"A very ticklish business, it was. Touch and go!"*
Beorn	12. *"A dozen! That's the first time I've heard eight called a dozen."*
Bilbo	13. *"I will give you a name and I shall call you Sting."*
Elvenking	14. *"There is no escape from my magic doors for those who are once brought inside."*
all the dwarves	15. *"We shall be bruised and battered to pieces, and drowned too, for certain!"*

MULTIPLE CHOICE: Choose the correct response and circle the answer. (1 point each)

1. The Took side of Bilbo's family was not as respectable as the Bagginses because:
   - **a.** They were part fairy.
   - **b.** They were poorer.
   - **(c.)** They were adventurous.

2. The dwarves were planning to:
   - **a.** visit their relatives in Moria
   - **(b.)** seek their treasure
   - **c.** fight goblins

3. Bill, Bert, and Tom kept these items in their lair:
   - **(a.)** supplies and treasures
   - **b.** sheep
   - **c.** prisoners

4. Elrond told the Company valuable information about:
   - **a.** how to fight dragons
   - **(b.)** the map and the swords
   - **c.** the spiders in Mirkwood

5. Thorin told the Great Goblin that they were traveling to:
   a. return home after a long absence
   b. win back treasure
   c. visit relatives

6. Gollum suggested a game of riddles in order to:
   a. learn about Bilbo
   b. to keep Bilbo's company
   c. to pass the time

7. Immediately after fleeing the mountain, the Company stumbled into:
   a. a party of elves
   b. a gathering of wolves
   c. an eagle's eyrie

8. Beorn came to like the dwarves because they:
   a. killed goblins
   b. came with Gandalf
   c. sang interesting songs

9. The dwarves were lured off the path in Mirkwood by:
   a. fear of spiders
   b. elvish magic
   c. hunger and desperation

10. The chief value in Bilbo's invisibility in the Elvenking's palace was that he was able to:
   a. steal food
   b. encourage the dwarves
   c. devise a plan of escape

VOCABULARY USAGE: Fill in the blank with the appropriate vocabulary word. (1 point each)

bulbous	eyrie	flummoxed	glowered	paraphernalia	precipice	purloined

1. The librarian glowered at the rowdy students as they noisily disrupted the quiet environment of the library. (v.)

2. The large bird's eyrie had been cleverly fashioned with twigs, grass, and mud. (n.)

3. The thief had to return each item he had purloined when he was caught red-handed by the store owner. (v.)

4. The man's bulbous nose was swollen and red as he sneezed into his handkerchief. (adj.)

5. Every year the baseball team hires a team manager to corral the various paraphernalia needed for each game. (n.)

6. The man was flummoxed when the doorbell rang, as he was not expecting any visitors. (adj.)

7. The base jumper stood precariously on the precipice as he eagerly awaited the signal to jump from his instructor. (n.)

ESSAY: Give good, complete answers, using full sentences and perfect punctuation. (5 points each)

1. Describe the two sides of Bilbo's personality or disposition as they relate to his mother's and father's sides of the family.

Important points:

- enjoys comfort and values sensible living without adventures; relates to the Bagginses
- fascinated by wonderful things and desires adventure; relates to the Tooks

Example:

Bilbo is from a respectable family among hobbits, the Bagginses, who are sensible, plain, and never do anything unexpected. He falls in line with this disposition in his family by enjoying a comfortable, commonplace life. On the other hand, there is an underlying Tookishness about him. The Took side of the family is known for adventures and is considered a bit queer by other hobbits. Bilbo is fascinated by wonderful things (e.g., Gandalf's fireworks, elves) and desires adventure.

2. Compare and contrast these three races: hobbits, dwarves, and elves.

Important points:

- hobbits: half man's height, relish comfort, and are skilled at going unnoticed
- dwarves: short, stout stature, with beards and a love of treasure
- elves: wise, noble, merry, fair

Example:

Hobbits are little people, about half a man's height. They relish comfort, and they are skilled at going unnoticed by other creatures. Dwarves are taller than hobbits, but shorter than men. They are stout and sturdy and grow long beards. At their heart is a love of gold, silver, gems, and all kinds of treasure. Elves look like men, and they are fair in appearance. While they are wise and noble, they are also merry-makers of songs and stories.

3. Tell how Bilbo has begun to prove these words of Gandalf: "I have chosen Mr. Baggins and that ought to be enough for all of you. … There is a lot more in him than you guess, and a deal more than he has any idea of himself."

Important points:

- tries to rob dangerous trolls
- escapes from Gollum and goblins in the mountain
- rescues the dwarves from spiders
- devises escape from Elvenking's prison

Example:

Bilbo proves there is more to him than meets the eye. He shows bravery in trying to rob a trio of dangerous trolls. Later he uses his wit to escape from Gollum and goblin guards under the mountain. He single-handedly rescues all the dwarves from being eaten by a horde of spiders, and soon after, he helps them escape from the Elvenking's prison.

Quiz 3: Chapters 10-14 — KEY

Name:______________________________ Date: ________________ Score: ________

MATCHING: Match the character to its correct description. (1 point each)

E 1. Lake-town
D 2. Dale
A 3. Master
G 4. Ravenhill
C 5. Front Gate
F 6. Bard
B 7. thrush

A. ruler of Lake-town; a shrewd and wary man
B. the large black bird that lives near the mountain
C. cavernous opening at Mountain's foot; source of Running River
D. a once-thriving town near the Mountain
E. a town on the surface of the Long Lake
F. a grim man descended from Lord Girion of Dale
G. a watch tower on the southern spur of the Mountain

MULTIPLE CHOICE: Use the map on the following page to answer the following questions. Circle the appropriate letter. (1 point each)

1. In the area labeled "A," which of the following occurs?
   - a. The Company rides in boats from the Elvenking's halls.
   - **(b.)** The dwarves and Bilbo are welcomed and aided by the men of Lake-town.
   - c. Gandalf joins the Company again.

2. In the area labeled "B," what does Bilbo do?
   - a. He leads the dwarves through the Front Gate.
   - **(b.)** He has a conversation with Smaug.
   - c. He shoots an arrow into the dragon's weak spot.

3. In the area labeled "A," who do we meet for the first time?
   - **(a.)** Bard
   - b. the Elvenking
   - c. Smaug the dragon

4. In the area labeled "B," which of the following is guarded?
   - a. the ring of invisibility
   - b. the crown of Durin
   - **(c.)** the Arkenstone

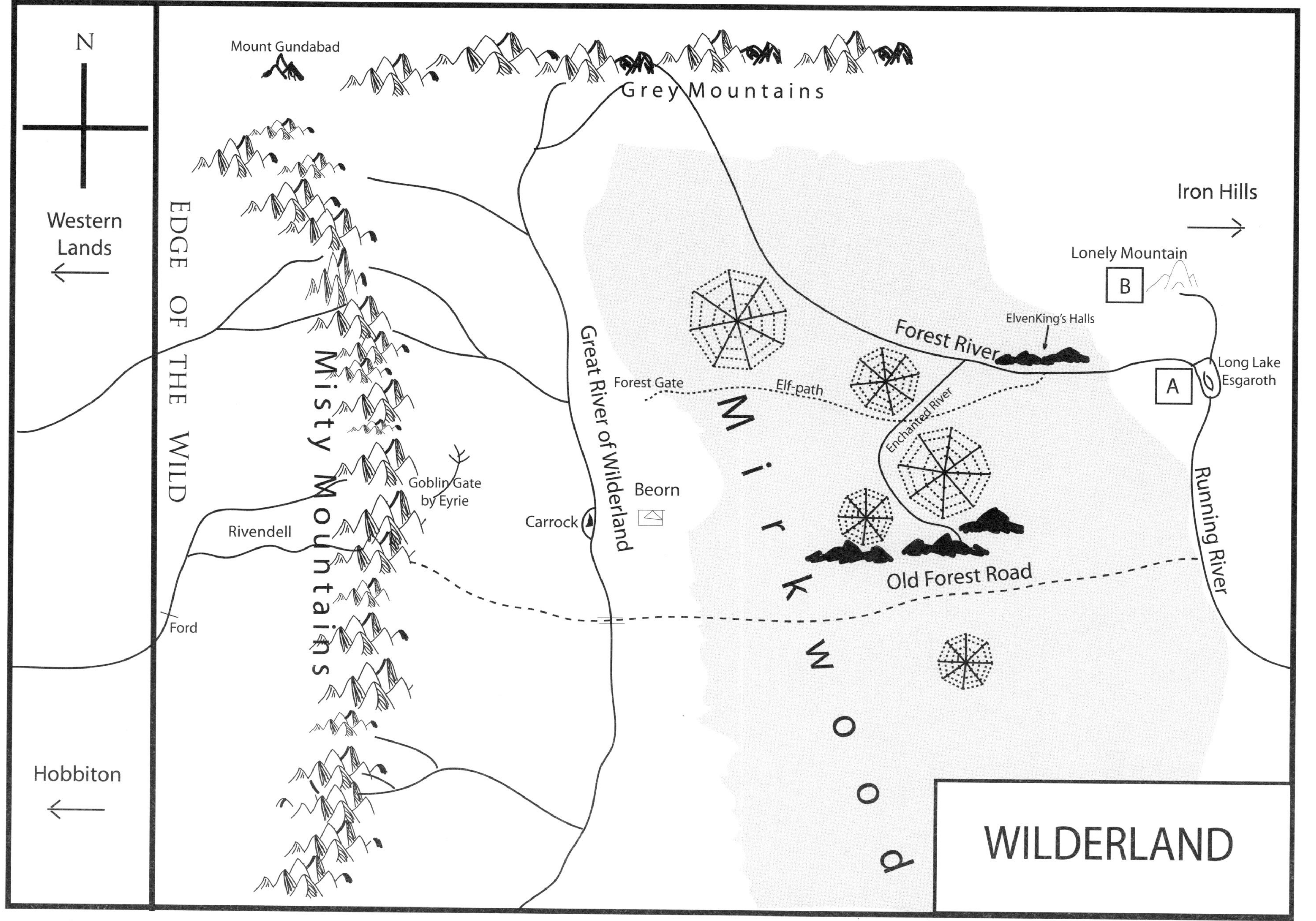
Mount Gundabad
Grey Mountains
Iron Hills
Lonely Mountain
B
ElvenKing's Halls
Forest River
A
Long Lake
Esgaroth
Running River
N
Western Lands
EDGE OF THE WILD
Misty Mountains
Forest Gate
Elf-path
Enchanted River
Mirkwood
Great River of Wilderland
Goblin Gate
by Eyrie
Beorn
Carrock
Old Forest Road
Rivendell
Ford
Hobbiton
WILDERLAND

COMPREHENSION QUESTIONS: Answer the following in complete sentences. (14 points total)

1. What methods do the dwarves use to attempt to open the door? Why do you think they are not successful? (3 pts.)

   They beat on it, push it, implore it to move, and say fragments of broken spells. They then use mining methods and tools. It is a magic door, and thus only opens by magic.

2. How does Bilbo trick Smaug into revealing his weak spot, and what is it? (4 pts.)

   Bilbo uses flattering talk, saying, "Lord Smaug the Impenetrable," and admiring his waistcoat of diamonds to trick Smaug into showing him his weak spot; he knows that Smaug will fall for it and give him a closer look at his belly. Smaug's weak spot is a large patch in the hollow of his left breast that is as bare as a snail out of its shell.

3. What does Bilbo find while searching through the treasure, what does he do with it, and what does he say about himself? (4 pts.)

   He finds the Arkenstone, hides it in his pocket, and withholds it from the dwarves; he calls himself a real burglar now.

4. What does the mere glimpse of the treasure rekindle in the hearts of the dwarves? Does this urge them on through the cavern? (3 pts.)

   It rekindles in the dwarves a fierceness and greed for their rediscovered treasure; yes, this urges them on.

Quiz 4: Chapters 15-19 — KEY

Name:______________________________ Date: ________________ Score: ______

MATCHING: Match the character to its correct description. (1 point each)

C 1. Roac

B 2. Dain

E 3. Dwarf and Goblin Wars

D 4. Bolg of the North

A 5. The Battle of Five Armies

A. a battle of goblins and wargs against men, elves, and dwarves

B. Thorin's cousin and chief of the dwarves of the Iron Hills

C. chief of the great ravens of the Mountain; son of Carc

D. goblin ruler whose father Dain had killed in the Goblin Wars

E. seven-year war in which dwarves hunted goblins

MULTIPLE CHOICE: Use the map on the following page to answer the following questions. Circle the appropriate letter. (1 point each)

1. Who comes from the area labeled "E"?

a. Dain and his army (circled)

b. Bolg and his army

c. the eagles

2. Who comes from the area labeled "C"?

a. Dain and his army

b. Bolg and his army (circled)

c. the eagles

3. In the area labeled "D," what occurs?

a. Bilbo kills many goblins and wargs.

b. Bilbo is knocked unconscious and the enemy doesn't notice him. (circled)

c. Bilbo loses the Arkenstone.

4. In the area labeled "B," what does Bilbo learn regarding Gandalf's absence?

a. that Gandalf had been gone fighting the Necromancer in Mirkwood. (circled)

b. that Gandalf was helping summon Dain for reinforcements.

c. that Gandalf was fighting large wicked spiders in Mirkwood.

5. In the area labeled "A," what has happened?

a. Trolls have invaded.

b. Bilbo has been presumed dead. (circled)

c. A search has begun for Bilbo.

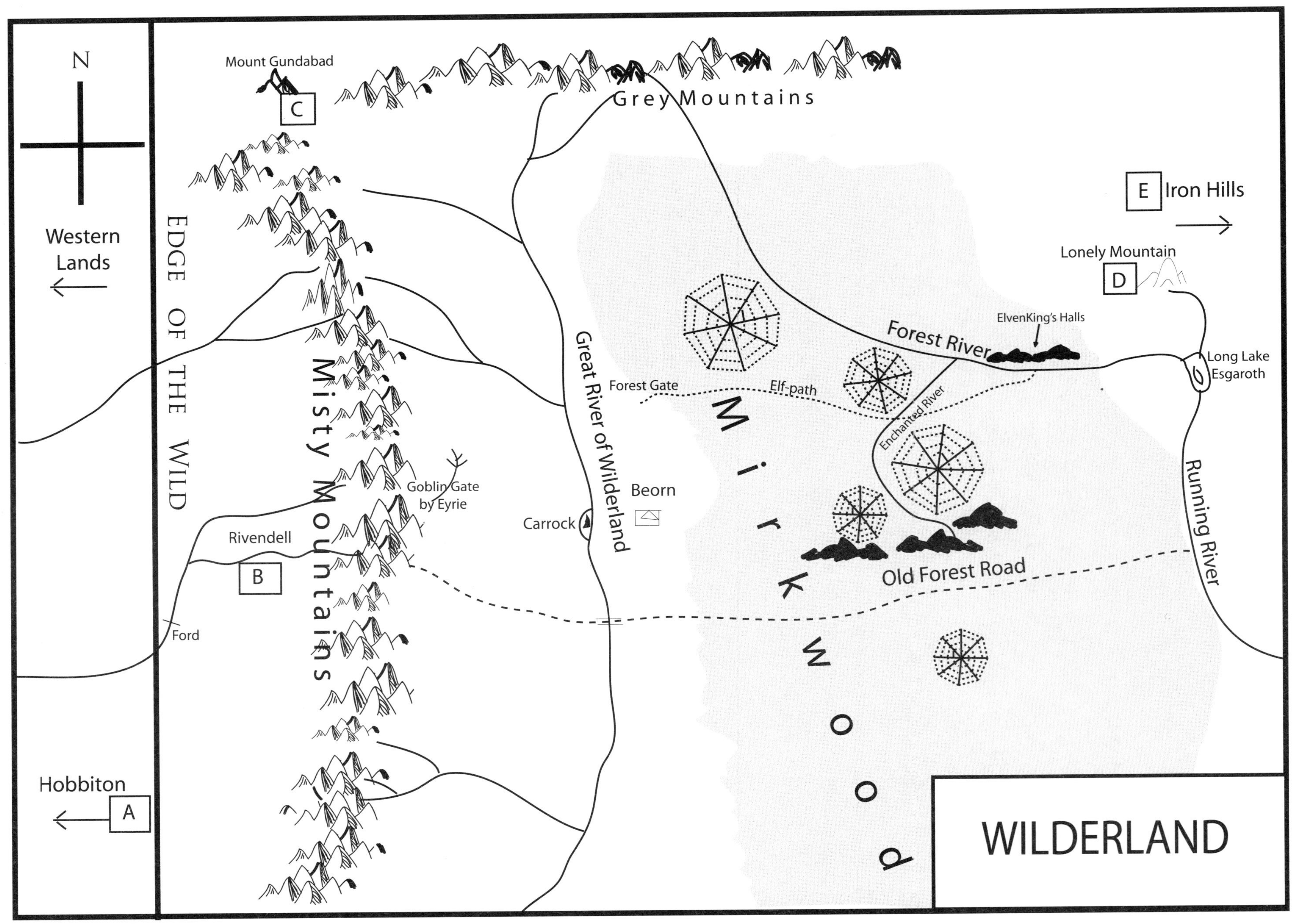
N
Western
Lands
Hobbiton
A
Mount Gundabad
C
Grey Mountains
EDGE OF THE WILD
Misty Mountains
Goblin Gate
by Eyrie
Rivendell
B
Ford
Carrock
Great River of Wilderland
Beorn
Forest Gate
Elf-path
Mirkwood
Forest River
ElvenKing's Halls
Enchanted River
Old Forest Road
E
Iron Hills
Lonely Mountain
D
Long Lake
Esgaroth
Running River
WILDERLAND

COMPREHENSION QUESTIONS: Answer the following in complete sentences. (15 points total)

1. Describe Roac. What is the message he delivers to Thorin? (3 pts.)

   He is a large black raven, a decrepit old bird, balding, getting blind; he tells Thorin about the death of Smaug, the gathering armies, and gives warning about the dwarves' treasure.

2. Thorin is obsessed with finding the Arkenstone. Where does Bilbo have it concealed, and how is it used when he negotiates with the enemy armies? (4 pts.)

   Bilbo has the Arkenstone wrapped in rags, and he is using it as a pillow. Bilbo is well received in the "enemy" camp, but the armies are unwilling to make peace, so Bilbo offers them the Arkenstone, which changes the discussion.

3. Who is waiting to say farewell to Bilbo? How does their meeting end? (4 pts.)

   Thorin is waiting to say farewell to Bilbo because he is dying and wants to apologize to Bilbo and thank him for his help. Bilbo weeps, and they part in kindness.

4. Where does Bilbo finally get a pocket-handkerchief? What meaning do you think the author intended for this little detail in the story? (4 pts.)

   Bilbo finally receives a red silk handkerchief from Elrond. This represents Bilbo's return to his comfortable life in Hobbiton, where handkerchiefs are necessary.

Final Exam: Chapters 10-19 — KEY

Name:______________________________ Date: ______________ Score: ______

WHO SAID IT?: Give the name of the speaker(s) for each quotation. (1 point each)

Bilbo 1. *"Well, are you alive or are you dead?"*

scouts of Lake-town 2. *"Who are you and what do you want?"*

Elvenking 3. *"Very well! We'll see! No treasure will come back through Mirkwood without my having something to say in the matter."*

Balin 4. *"There lies all that is left of Dale."*

Bombur 5. *"I am too fat for such fly-walks. I should turn dizzy and tread on my beard, and then you would be thirteen again."*

Bilbo 6. *"You said sitting on the doorstep and thinking would be my job ..."*

Smaug 7. *"Well, thief! I smell you and I feel your air."*

Bilbo 8. *"Never laugh at live dragons!"*

Thorin 9. *"The Arkenstone! The Arkenstone!"*

Smaug 10. *"They shall see me and remember who is the real King under the Mountain!"*

Thorin 11. *"Now what on earth or under it has happened?"*

Thorin 12. *"Don't call my palace a nasty hole! You wait till it has been cleaned and redecorated!"*

Bard 13. *"The dragon is coming or I am a fool!"*

the townspeople 14. *"Up the Bowman, and down with Moneybags!"*

Thorin 15. *"You put your worst cause last and in the chief place."*

Bilbo 16. *"I would give a good deal for the feel of grass at my toes."*

Gandalf 17. *"Well done! Mr. Baggins! There is always more about you than anyone expects!"*

Gandalf 18. *"If you don't like my Burglar, please don't damage him."*

Thorin 19. *"You all seem in league! What have you got to say, you descendant of rats?"*

Elvenking 20. *"Long will I tarry, ere I begin this war for gold."*

Bilbo 21. *"The eagles are coming!"*

Thorin 22. *"There is more in you of good than you know, child of the kindly West."*

Bard 23. *"There let it lie till the Mountain falls!"*

elves of Rivendell 24. *"And your snores would waken a stone dragon."*

Gandalf 25. *"My dear Bilbo! Something is the matter with you! You are not the hobbit that you were."*

MULTIPLE CHOICE: Choose the correct response and circle the answer. (1 point each)

1. The first dwarf out of his barrel was recognized by his:
   - a. blue hood, silver belt
   - b. white beard, scarlet hood
   - **c.** sky-blue hood, gold chain

2. Most people in Lake-town thought the dwarves were:
   - a. vagabonds and tramps
   - **b.** fulfilling a prophecy
   - c. lying about their story

3. When they could not open the secret door, the dwarves:
   - **a.** blamed Bilbo
   - b. went in the Front Gate
   - c. decided to give up

4. Bilbo remembered the message of the runes because:
   - **a.** a thrush appeared
   - b. the moon shone
   - c. a pebble fell on his head

5. When Bilbo went down the tunnel toward Smaug, it was:
   - a. damp and clammy
   - **b.** his bravest act
   - c. blocked by fallen stone

6. Bilbo stole this on his first visit to Smaug:
   - a. the Arkenstone
   - b. silver armor
   - **c.** a cup

7. Looking at Smaug's waistcoat of diamonds, Bilbo saw:
   - a. the Arkenstone
   - **b.** a weak spot
   - c. an impenetrable defense

8. When Bilbo found the Arkenstone, he:
   - a. gave it to Thorin
   - **b.** put it in his pocket
   - c. hid it under a rock

9. The dwarves and Bilbo were in the Mountain for:
   - a. a whole day and a night
   - b. five days
   - **c.** two nights and a day

10. Because his treasure had been thieved, Smaug blamed:
    - **a.** the men of Lake-town
    - b. the elves of Mirkwood
    - c. the dwarves of Esgaroth

11. The Elvenking gathered his army to march for:
    - a. an attack on Smaug
    - b. the rebuilding of Lake-town
    - **c.** the Mountain

12. This person told Thorin about the death of Smaug and the gathering of armies:
    - **a.** Roac
    - b. Carc
    - c. Cram

13. Thorin sent messengers to Dain hoping for help to:
    - a. carry away the treasure
    - b. fight off goblins
    - **c.** guard the gold for themselves

14. Bilbo's displeasure with the situation between Thorin and Bard forced him to:
    - a. call Gandalf to his aid
    - **b.** give away the Arkenstone
    - c. go back home

15. The Elvenking did not want:

- **a.** to fight over gold (circled)
- **b.** to let the dwarves win
- **c.** Bilbo to fight in battle

16. The turning point of the battle was:

- **a.** the onslaught of wargs
- **b.** Thorin's entry
- **c.** the eagles' arrival (circled)

17. When Bilbo was found, Gandalf took him to:

- **a.** see Thorin (circled)
- **b.** get food and drink
- **c.** rest in the camp

18. A chest of silver and a chest of gold were given to:

- **a.** Dain
- **b.** Bilbo (circled)
- **c.** the Elvenking

19. Gandalf had left the Company at the gate to Mirkwood in order to:

- **a.** warn the wood-men
- **b.** fight the Necromancer (circled)
- **c.** learn from the White Council

20. Upon arriving back in Hobbiton, Bilbo found that he had lost:

- **a.** his best set of forks
- **b.** his magic ring
- **c.** most of the hobbits' respect (circled)

FILL IN THE BLANK: Fill in the blank with the correct word. (1 point each)

1. The dwarves came out of the barrels once they arrived at ___Lake-town___.
2. The ___Master___ of Lake-town helped the dwarves, but hoped they'd leave.
3. When the Company left Lake-town, the only gloomy person was ___Bilbo___.
4. From the Front Gate of the Lonely Mountain runs the ___Running___ River.
5. The town in ruins that stands near the Mountain was called ___Dale___.
6. The secret door was found by Fili, Kili, and ___Bilbo___.
7. Bilbo called himself Ringwinner, Luckwearer, and ___Barrel___-rider.
8. Smaug could not see Bilbo because of the magic ___ring___.
9. The Arkenstone was known as the ___Heart___ of the Mountain.
10. Thorin dressed ___Bilbo___ in a coat of silver-steel called mithril.
11. The warning of Smaug's attack on Lake-town was sounded by ___Bard___.
12. The Master blamed the ___dwarves___ for Smaug's attack.
13. The ___Elvenking___ and his army stopped to help the men of Lake-town rebuild.
14. Thorin's cousin living in the Iron Hills was ___Dain___.

15. Bard argued with Thorin to give some of the treasure to men and elves.

16. Thorin was kept from throwing Bilbo off the wall by Gandalf.

17. Bolg of the North attacked the Mountain with goblins and wargs.

18. Beorn killed the goblin chief and ensured the victory.

19. On the return journey, Gandalf and Bilbo visited Elrond's home, Rivendell.

20. The old Master had caught the dragon-sickness and come to a bad end.

VOCABULARY USAGE: Fill in the blank with the appropriate vocabulary word. (1 point each)

antiquated	lore	implored	glowered	eyrie	flummoxed	promontory
purloined	precipice	pallid	succoured	bulbous	deposed	paraphernalia

1. The medic succoured the wounded, even in the most dangerous of circumstances. (v.)

2. The fans glowered as they watched their favorite sports team lose the game to their rival. (v.)

3. The clothing exhibit in the museum modeled antiquated styles from the 1800s. (adj.)

4. The young boy's face turned pallid as the menacing dog came closer. (adj.)

5. Darting its bulbous eyes back and forth, the chameleon quickly changed color to avoid being seen by the predator. (adj.)

6. The ruler was deposed as a result of his unjust and immoral practices. (v.)

7. The aged lighthouse stood at the end of a long promontory overlooking the sea. (n.)

8. While hiking, a group of adventurous teenagers stumbled upon an abandoned eyrie that clearly had been home to a large bird. (n.)

9. Any retelling of Greek mythological lore must include the story of Perseus killing the Gorgon, Medusa. (n.)

10. Before going to bed, the girl collected the necessary paraphernalia for the next day's activities. (n.)

11. The student, flummoxed by the verb endings, could not accurately conjugate the verb. (adj.)

12. Though strictly commanded by the general not to, the soldier purloined gold, silver, and a beautiful garment during the attack on the enemy's city. (v.)

13. With tears in her eyes, the little girl implored her dad to reconsider letting her have a puppy for her birthday. (v.)

14. Standing on the precipice of the Grand Canyon, the tourist was able to see a vast panorama of beauty. (n.)

ESSAY: Give good, complete answers, using full sentences and perfect punctuation. (5 points each)

1. Compare and contrast Bard and the Master; how are they alike, how are they different?

Important points:

- Alike: leadership abilities and desire; suspicious of others
- Different: Bard is brave, puts the needs of the people before himself, and does not let gold rule him. The Master acts cowardly, puts himself first, and covets money.

Example:

Bard and the Master are similar and also different. They both desire to lead and are capable of the job. They are also not overly trusting of others, and they regard strangers with suspicion. Their differences are stark. Bard shows bravery and selflessness as he fights the dragon and aids the people of Lake-town, while the Master tries to escape during the attack, and later calls servants to attend to his needs first. The Master desires gold chiefly for himself, while Bard willingly gives to others.

2. Describe the effect that the dragon's enchanted hoard had on Bilbo, Thorin, and the old Master of Lake-town.

Important points:

- Bilbo: amazed by it and wants it at first, but gets over it
- Thorin: turns him to greed and almost destroys friendship with Bilbo
- Master: leads him to take most of the gold for himself and he dies of starvation

Example:

The enchanted gold amazed Bilbo at first, but he soon desired the comforts of home over treasure. Thorin was affected more greatly, as the treasure turned him to greed and war, and it almost ruined his friendship with Bilbo. The Master came under the dragon-spell worst of all. He took most of the treasure meant for the people and fled into the wasteland, where he died of starvation.

3. At the end of the story, Gandalf says, "You are a very fine person, Mr. Baggins, and I am very fond of you; but you are only quite a little fellow in a wide world after all!" Bilbo responds by saying, "Thank goodness!" and laughs happily. Why is Gandalf's comment not a put-down but an encouragement?

Important points:

- Gandalf likes Bilbo and tells him he's a fine person.
- The good turnout of the adventure was not up to luck, nor was it all up to Bilbo.

Example:

Gandalf's comment is not a put-down because he tells of his fondness for Bilbo and says he is a very fine person. His words are, in fact, an encouragement. Bilbo might be tempted to think that the good turnout of the adventure was brought about by his good luck alone. Gandalf's words remind him, however, that things are not up to chance or the skills of a little fellow like Bilbo. Knowing this is an encouragement and a relief to Bilbo.